LONDON

ILLUSTRATED
GEOLOGICAL WALKS

Eric Robinson

Book One

Photographs by Mike Gray
Maps by Colin Stuart

Published to Celebrate
the 125th Anniversary
of
The Geologists' Association

by

Scottish Academic Press
Edinburgh and London

LONDON
ILLUSTRATED GEOLOGICAL WALKS

Published by
Scottish Academic Press Ltd.
33 Montgomery Street, Edinburgh EH7 5JX
for the
Geologists' Association

ISBN 0 7073 0350 8

© 1984 Eric Robinson

Printed in Northern Ireland by
The Universities Press (Belfast) Ltd.

INTRODUCTION

This book has several aims. The first of these is to demonstrate that geology can be taken up and explored for the first time through the building stones of city streets. When granites and marbles are cut and polished to be fitted to buildings, they provide us with unique opportunities to study textures and mineral compositions which would never be available to us in weathered, natural outcrops. For this reason, it is easier to instruct beginners in Geology using shop fronts or wall surfaces than by taking them to scattered crags or insecure quarry faces.

A second purpose is to remind experienced geologists of the diversity of rock types available to them in cities, and of the fact that dated buldings allow them to assess weathering and natural decay in well-known rock types. In this last field, there are greater opportunities to be precise about the durability of stone than would ever be possible from laboratory experiments or from the study of natural outcorps.

A third aim brings us into the field of Industrial Archaeology and is simply to record changes in the use of different rock types, and to a lesser extent, changing methods of building and construction. The 19th century saw a departure from reliance on purely British stone. Improved transport made it easier to import granites from Scandinavia and marble from Mediterranean countries. These patterns in turn have now been modified by trade with more distant parts of the World. Brazil and India are the latest regions to contribute to the colours and textural range of the streets of London.

With the city now being an open air museum for Geology, a fourth aim is to make a lasting record of the stones of particular buildings. Any reasonably competent geologist can attempt to identify stone in a building from first principles, and may in this way get close to the truth. Sometimes the truth can be verified from written records, word-of-mouth, or a matching of specimens. Surprisingly, there is a shortage of facts in the architectural accounts of buildings, both in the matter of recording what the rock is, and where it came from. Colour, and broad general terms such as 'granite' or 'marble' are used. These terms may only mean that the rock is hard or can take and retain a polish. Often this is as much as we will get from the literature of architecture. In this situation, it is an important purpose to persuade that there is a need to record the geological details as much as the furnishings and fittings which are normally exhaustively catalogued.

A fifth aim must be to advocate a central record of rock types used in buildings. In a perfect World, information would be formally filed with a National Building Record, but understaffed and underfinanced, the existing branch of the Department of the Environment can only cope with some part of its historic buildings responsibility let alone attend to the recent past or present. As much is true of the British Geological Survey as it contemplates decentralisation from its long-established London base.

A sixth and final aim for this book is a practical one—to respond to the growing popularity of geological walks in the City. It is now some six years since *The Geologists' Association* added city walks to their programme of outdoor meetings on Saturdays or Sunday afternoons when traffic is less pressing. What was discovered at the time, and research details that were uncovered in response to questions asked during the walks, have become the basis of the text which follows. These walks allow others to follow the itineraries at their own speed and to the limit of their interest on the day, not forgetting the scope to modify and improve upon the information offered.

Happily, publication coincides with the 125th anniversary of the founding of *The Geologists' Association*. The book is dedicated to the Association's aim of providing a geological experience to the Amateur. In 1858, the G.A. pointed to the half-day outing into the countryside around London as an entry to the World of Geology. Today, we direct those seeking Geology to the streets of the City, with the reminder that there, Geology is all around you.

Initially, it is necessary to make genuine acknowledgement to all the

Architectural Historians for their invariable omission of sound and honest geology from their accounts of buildings. This has always been the stimulus to the work in hand. Having said this, it would be only fair to admit considerable debt to Professor Pevsner for his volume dealing with the City in the Penguin series, 'The Buildings of England'. With so much historical fact and guidance towards the significant features of the hundreds of buildings which he lists, his survey provided the structure upon which the geological 'clothes' are hung. Second only to Pevsner must be the milestone in conservation, the book 'Save the City' which set up so many worthy causes after its publication in 1976.

The whole idea of geological walks as used in this book was 'borrowed' from the guide published by Ian Simpson and Fred Broadhurst for Central Manchester in 1975, combining architectural observations with geological facts within the limits of a continuous walked itinerary. The pattern of the earliest walk was shaped with the valued assistance of Dr Clive Bishop, before other duties took up his time. When it comes to geological details, over the years, many people have volunteered facts and observations which I have gratefully accepted. Much came from conversations on-site with stone-fitters and members of the trade. Of these, I would like to mention Mr. A. Bannock of Bannocks of Birmingham, Mr. Fecitt of Kirkstone Green Slate, and Mr. Derrick Rice of Cumbria Stone, for direct answers to questions on the mysteries of trade names for marbles and granites. Equally helpful were many Architects, who either talked from their recollections of buildings or sought details from the specifications at the time of construction. For their comments on the ground, when confronted by buildings, thanks are due to Frank Dimes, John Dangerfield and Alan Nicholson, who are all specialists in their own right on various aspects of stone work or rock types.

A considerable debt is owed to Mike Gray, photographer in the Department of Geology, University College London, for his flair in viewing buildings in their context and producing prints appropriate to the text as well as of artistic merit. Equally important have been the efforts of Colin Stuart, cartographer of the same Department, in devising the street maps which hold together the twisting itineraries.

References

Lloyd, D. 1976 *Save the City—a conservation study of the City of London,* SPAB, 1-196.

Simpson, I. and Broadhurst, F. 1975 *A Building Stones Guide to Central Manchester,* Dept. Extra-Mural Studies, Manchester, 1-39.

Cannon Street from St Paul's

ST PAUL'S CATHEDRAL AND ITS PRECINCT

There are few better starting points for a geological walk in the City of London than the top of the steps outside the West Front of St Paul's Cathedral. The cathedral itself is, amongst other things, a monument to that significant choice by Wren of stone from the Isle of Portland for the rebuilding after The Great Fire of 1666. From this bold beginning followed the whole and dramatic transformation of almost all the City churches in the later 17th century. In turn, this produced the continued use of the same white limestone for Banks, Insurance Offices, Civic Buildings, or indeed any building where there is the need to impress the Public of worth and reliability through the quality and appearance of the fabric (Summerson, 1976).

We begin by standing at the top of the steps, within the portico fronted by the massive flutted columns. The paving here is a chequerboard of black and white marble squares, the white probably being Italian and from the quarries around Carrara in the northern Apennines. The contrasting black marble is really a muddy limestone either from quarries close to Tournai in Belgium or from the west of Ireland. Being dense and compact, the dark limestone does take a polish; so technically to the trade it would be classed as a 'marble' although lacking the metamorphic history which a geologist would expect with that rock name. There are no diagnostic fossils here to prove the matter of age conclusively, but such is not the case for the large slabs which form the topmost step to the frontage and also the bases to the massive columns of the portico. Polished and hollowed out by the tread of feet over two centuries, this equally dark stone does contain tiny crinoid ossicles and finely broken shell fragments which prove it to be a muddy variety of Carboniferous Limestone.

It would have been satisfying to have been able to confirm a traditional story that the 'black marble' was the gift of the Bishop of Sodor and Man of building stone from his See at the time of the rebuilding, but sadly this stone seems in no way comparable with the well-known Poyllvaaish Black Marble of the island. The whole background to this story has been satisfactorily explored by Eva Wilson (*G.A. Circulars* 823 and 825, 1981) from records in Manx Customs documents as well as her personal knowledge of the rock types involved. Her conclusion is that the black earthy limestone probably came from the Dublin district, probably from a quarry referred to as 'at the Red Cow near Dublin' by the 18th century writer Rutty (1772). The Manx confusion may have stemmed from the fact that the stone could have been dressed and finished in the Isle of Man before being delivered to St Paul's. By an ironic twist, the legend may have prompted the use of genuine Manx limestone in other parts of St Paul's in the course of late-19th century renovations (Wilson, *Circular* 823). Whatever the source of the limestone of the present-day top step, the wearing qualities were poor and in all probability necessitated replacement in late-Victorian times by the present 2 m lengths of axe-dressed dark blue diorite, a tough, durable igneous rock. This stone has two aspects here; unworn, it has a rough matt surface which reveals very little of the internal structures. Polished by foot tread, however, the same rock shows a colour-mottling which gives some idea of the clustering of the dark mineral components (pyroxenes and iron ores) and the contrasting light minerals (mainly feldspars). This rock differs from granite in its lack of the pale mineral quartz, and for this reason is termed a 'basic' igneous rock. This particular rock and its source have once again been the subject of some discussion, with a certain measure of 'traditional tale' coming into the identification of diorite from quarries on Guernsey in the Channel Islands. Dr David Keen recalls being told when mapping on Guernsey that 'granite' from northern Guernsey had been used in the steps of St Paul's. Indeed, a lady had gone so far as to point out the very quarry in the area of St Sampson's. In fact this importation fits very well with an established pattern of trade in Victorian times. Guernsey blue-grey diorite provided much of the stone for London kerbs and cobbles, as well as the broad steps of Carlton House Terrace leading up to the Duke of York's Column (Herm Diorite).

West Front of St Paul's from Juxon House

Below the upper flight of diorite steps, the broad platform surface at mid-level is enlivened by squares of red and grey limestone set within a framework of white Italian Marble. Both red and grey rocks are from the same source, the island of Öland off the Baltic Coast of Sweden. The rock is part of the Ordovician Orthoceras Limestone, a fact amply proved by the frequent examples of the tapered and chambered shells of the named fossil which are evident, particularly on the grey-blue slabs (*Orthoceras* is a straight-shelled cephalopod, distantly related to the modern *Nautilus*). Many of these slabs are cut across the natural bedding of the limestone so that the stratification is picked out for us by colour banding. Some layers show evidence of erosion immediately following the deposition of the sediment on the sea bottom. The upper sections of what should be complete cylindrical cross-sections of *Orthoceras* have been scoured away. This kind of evidence in a field outcrop would afford an excellent indication of what was the 'top' surface of a bed. In contrast, the red slabs seem to have been split paral-

Rock types of St Paul's West Front steps & paving.
  A: Black and white marble paving
  B: Diorite of steps and surround
  C: Swedish Öland Limestone
  D: Cornish Granite
  E: Purbeck Limestone setts
  F: Carrara Marble
  G: Sharp Granite bollards

Panels of Swedish Limestone, West Front.

lel to bedding, so that they show a pattern of roughly polygonal cracks (filled by grey mud) which represents periods of desiccation and drying out of the mud surface, followed by a subsequent re-flooding by sediment of a different colour. This reflects the known history of early Ordovician sedimentation in the Baltic—a period of alternating rise and fall of sea-level in what must have been a shallow shelf sea.

At the bottom of the lower flight of diorite steps, the smooth paved area at street level is floored by flags of a pale grey granite rich in elongate lath-shaped feldspar crystals which, from their swirling pattern of alignments give a vivid impression of fluid movement before the whole melt solidified into this characteristic igneous rock. The texture and the colour, all suggest that this is in fact a Cornish Granite, possibly from Bodmin Moor. Precise identification would depend upon the study of a thin section of the rock and its comparison with known standards.

In front of the granite paving, further slabs of the same granite outline some twenty square areas which contain edge-on blocks of Purbeck Limestone set diagonally to the granite framework. Two types of limestone are present; one is the well-known shelly variety that is often polished to a marble finish (Purbeck Marble). Its distinctive appearance being created by the small gastropods which crowd the beds; the other limestone is the

tufa-like, cavity-rich rock which we see in the cliffs at Swanage. Fossils are notably absent from this limestone, which, like other Upper Jurassic rocks from this part of the Dorset coast, may have been formed in rather special lagoonal conditions, too saline for rich shell life.

At the focal point of the paved area stands the statue of Queen Anne, set up to celebrate the completion of the rebuilding within her reign. The original statue, the work of Francis Bird, was completed in finest Italian Marble (1712). It suffered so badly in the sulphurous atmosphere of 18th century London that it had to be replaced by the present replica (in Italian Statuary Marble) in 1886. This type of marble has a distinctive hue (either a sour-milk blue, or a yellowish grey) and an equally distinctive surface weathering. This results in the 'goose-pimple' effect on the allegoric figures (figures representing Ireland, America, India and France) that are grouped about the pedestal. In our climate, Italian Marble tends to develop a dusty white surface of loose grains of calcite which can be brushed off with the hand as a fine white sand. Around the base of the statue, the radially arranged setts are once again blocks of Purbeck Limestone.

Limestone setts, West Front.

Completing the geology of the cathedral West Front, one of the most splendid features of the whole

4

design is the semicircle of substantial bollards of highly polished Shap Granite which help to keep the area clear of parked cars and coaches. The stone is from the quarries on Wasdale Crag close to the A6 road as it crosses Shap Fell in the south east Lake District. As distinct from the nearby grey Cornish Granite, the texture of Shap Granite combines prominent large pink orthoclase feldspar crystals, set in a finer grained, reddish-brown groundmass, the whole representing an example of the rock type known as porphyry. Such strongly figured rocks were sought in antiquity and fashioned into bowls, vases and pedestals by the Egyptians, Greeks and Romans.

In another historic sense, Shap Granite will always be famous in the history of Geology as a science for the interpretation of the dark clots of material which sometimes blemish the even colour tone of the surfaces. These xenoliths (literally, 'foreign stones') more vividly called 'heathen' by the quarrymen, are actually blocks of the country rock into which the granite was injected. They were dislodged and incorporated into the granite itself in a process of digestion. This is how we interpret the situation today, but in the 18th century, in one of the most celebrated debates in geology the case had to be argued for a hot molten origin for granite as against the notion that granite crystallised from an aqueous solution. Decisive evidence in this discussion was precisely similar to what we can see here in these bollards that some of the same large pink orthoclase crystals of the granite are to be found 'grown' within the dark mass of the xenoliths. The second of the smaller bollards to the west of the larger bollards which mark the carriage entrance to the cathedral, on the north side of the frontage, is the best example you could find anywhere of the proof for the molten origin for granites. As a colour contrast, these bollards spring from base slabs which are of the same diorite which we have seen in the steps. As it happens, this rock too has included fragments of country rock within its mass; in this case, the material is clearly banded slate which is the prevailing rock type of South West England and Brittany, including the intervening Channel Islands.

The replacement of the Queen Anne statue and indeed the whole

Shap Granite bollard, West Front.

design of the paved area of the West Front, which we have just analysed, are very much the result of a late-19th century reconstruction of space which had previously become something of a public disgrace. The ground was in fact part of the overgrown churchyard of St Paul's, extending up to railings which narrowed down the busy thoroughfare of Ludgate Hill. Not only did this create traffic congestion on a busy street, but it also hindered the planned development of an improved water supply and mains drainage to this part of the City. For many years the authorities argued with the Dean and Chapter over their rights to open up enclosed ground. Such permissions were finally agreed in 1874, after which date there commenced the planning of the West Front as we have described it above. The diversity of rock types which has been our satisfaction is in fact very typical for Victorian times, when stone was drawn from the widest range of sources to achieve colour and textural contrasts desired by architects and planners.

Returning now to the Cathedral itself, the outer shell of the building is of Portland Stone and the varying surface textures and colour tones which it shows reflect the differential weathering of the limestone as it has been exposed to a polluted atmosphere for over two centuries of time. The exposed surfaces (west facing for the most-part) tend to have weathered whitest; the more protected areas stand out darker in contrast. Why this should be, in scientific terms is not at all clear. Prior to 1973, the contrasts were further emphasised by the black encrustations of soot and grime which have since been removed through extensive cleaning operations. It has been a source of much disappointment to the cleaning lobby among conservationists, that the outcome of treatments in some areas has been at best a yellow surface rather than the gleaming whiteness of naturally weathered Portland Stone. The penetration of the air-borne tars and polluting carbons has evidently been deep. An understanding of the weathering of natural stone in city atmospheres and what can be done to counter discolouration and surface decay, is a field of research which is only in its infancy.

Scanning the surfaces of the large blocks at head height in the West Front, you quickly become aware of a number of processes which have effected the stonework. There is a crazed skin of sulphate, almost inert to drops of dilute hydrochloric acid so proving its non-carbonate nature. In places, this hard skin erupted into unsightly blisters which when ruptured, expose fresh limestone surfaces to attack. Very little can be done to eradicate such blemishes short of rubbing down the surfaces or cutting out and replacing whole areas of stone. Yet another type of weathering can be seen at what were the sharply dressed corners and edges to blocks. Here, curving, shell-like fractures which tend to round off the angles are the result of frost action involving the freezing and thawing of pore moisture in this semi-permeable stone. In these details, it is interesting to compare the older stonework of St Paul's with the same limestone in the Edwardian buildings of St Paul's Churchyard opposite, or in the even more recent cladding slabs to **Juxon House** to the north (**1**).

Beneath the weathering skin, all the white limestone of the Cathedral is the even-grained, almost non-shelly limestone which is quarried from the thicker bed units of the Portland quarries, beds of up to $1\frac{1}{2}$–2 m thickness, often with more shelly top and bottom layers which are trimmed away from the solid core to the stone bed. Each bed, both thick and thin, tends to have its own distinctive name to the quarrymen. The principal source of 'dimension' stone from Portland is either the Base-Bed or the Whit-Bed in quarryman's nomenclature. If you can see a freshly cleaned or broken surface and study it with a low magnification hand lens, you will realise that the limestone is made up of regular sized rounded grains which pack together tightly to give the stone its compact texture. As there are no strong planes of weakness such as bedding within the rock, it is one which the mason or sculptor can dress in almost any direction with equal ease. For this reason, Portland Stone such as we see here, is one of the natural stones which can be termed a 'freestone'. It was a thoroughly suitable material for the rich stone carving of Wren's master-masons. We shall see much of Portland Stone in the course of our walks, stone of all ages and maturity, with further characteristics to note as they arise. What remains impressive is the consistent quality of it all.

To begin our walk, we can do no better than to take the Queen Anne statue as our starting point. To the north, there is the extensive complex of offices and shopping arcades which represent the completion of Sir William Holford's plan for the north precinct area, initiated in 1956 and completed in 1965. The closest of the several component units is **Juxon House** (**1**), a modern building, steel-framed and with panels of stone attached as cladding. The principal cladding material is Portland Stone, again probably the smooth textured Whit-Bed of the Dorset quarries. While the stone overall is free from obvious fossil shell, the surfaces have a roughness to the touch which stems from tiny broken fragments of oyster and bivalve shell. These have emerged through surface weathering from what was a smoothly dressed surface in the 1960's. Portland Stone is indeed a bioclastic limestone.

Between the narrow buttress strips of Portland Stone which run down the entire face of the frontage, are tile-like pieces of blue-grey slate which contrast effectively with the smoothness and the colour of the Jurassic limestone. The stone is Burlington Slate from quarries in the Silurian age Bannisdale Slates of the southern Lake District, probably from the fells above the Duddon Estuary.

Juxon House from West Front.

Only part of that succession would provide the thin fissile beds suitable for roofing slate, the greater part of the succession being of coarser grain and producing slate-slabstone with a less perfect cleavage such as we see here. If we look closely at some of these slates, a faint colour banding will catch the eye running across the surfaces. This is the sedimentary bedding of the rock and is quite at variance with the direction of splitting of the slate, which is termed cleavage. Cleavage is a structure within the rock which is produced by pressure and deformation causing a realignment of the flakey and platy minerals at right angles to the stress. In the Burlington Slates, the pressures which produced the Lake District mountains were equally responsible for this cleavage which cuts across the natural bedding of the original rock.

In addition to these sedimentary rocks of one kind or another, Juxon House is crossed by panels of pale grey granite at first floor level where it is not too easy to identify. Even-grained, it could be either Cornish or one of the granites from the Southern Uplands of Scotland, but its provenance is unknown. As much is true for the very different 'Black Granite' which we see at pavement level in the frontages of the shops and offices of Juxon House. We shall have several debates as to the nature and source of these black granites in the course of our walks. The reason is that under this one

descriptive name (for all are admittedly 'black') there is grouped a multitude of different rock types. Fundamentally, however, they all have it in common that they are rocks which have been altered to some degree from their original character. This alteration is the result of mineralisation whereby clear, colourless minerals such as the feldspars (probably the principal rock-forming minerals), become crowded with grains of magnetite and other opaque ores to such an extent that light is no longer freely reflected, and the dark, sombre hues are produced. If the original rock was poor in silica, the dark tone can be intense. This is the fate of basalts and some gabbros. If on the other hand, the rock was quartz-bearing (such as granite), the resulting end product could be a paler, more-mottled 'Black Granite'. Most if not all 'Black Granites' come from ancient continent core areas of the World, usually of Precambrian age so that there have been long spans of time in which the alterations can have built up in the building stone we see here.

Turning specifically to the rock of Juxon House, this particular 'Black Granite' shows a characteristic mottling of grey and black which is recognisable as being Rustenberg Gabbro from quarries outside Pretoria in South Africa—part of the very large Bushveld Igneous Complex formed mainly of basic and ultrabasic rocks. If we look at these slabs slightly against the light, it is possible

7

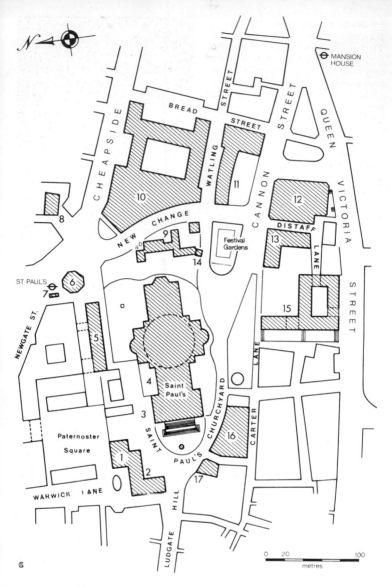

Numbers on the map identify buildings in the text.

to make out the outlines of feldspar laths as they have been picked out by delicate screens of metallic ore in the replacement process mentioned above. Total replacement has produced the workable chromite deposits of this same area of the Transvaal.

Parts of Juxon House are the premises of **Barclays Management Services** (**2**), the entrance foyer to which has walls lined by large panels of the Italian Marble, Grigio Fiorito Timau. This is a grey limestone of Devonian age from the province of Udine in northeast Italy. From its

involvement in the uplift and folding of the Julian Alps, it has been deformed and cut through by countless veins of white calcite, producing the distinctive grey and white pattern of this rock. As with all strongly figured marbles, the stonefitters have taken the orientation of the veining in this rock and produced mirror-image symmetry patterns to good effect.

Walking now past the north side of St Paul's and past Bancroft House which is the 'twin' of Juxon House, notice the broad flagstone of the paved area (and indeed, the whole

Precinct) as examples of what is popularly called York Stone (**3**). These 5–7 cm thick slabs of micaceous sandstone are cut from larger blocks quarried from the Coal Measure successions of West Yorkshire. The quarries are well away from the City of York itself, and are concentrated rather in that triangle between Leeds, Bradford and Huddersfield which includes the towns of Elland and Brighouse. When freshly cut, the rock is pale and yellow, but as it weathers the iron minerals cementing the sand grains oxidise causing the stone to darken in tone, eventually and naturally turning black, even in the cleanest air. It is a popular fallacy to regard blackness as a consequence and a measure of pollution, indeed, this has been the pretext for much unnecessary cleaning of buildings in the north of England where blackness could have been counted enhancing to Victorian buildings. Some of the flags here in the Precinct retain the wire cut marks of their working in the quarry, testifying to the hardwearing qualities of the tone. Equally important for paving must be its non-slip wearing characteristice—a stone which became smoother with foot-tread could be positively dangerous.

Halfway across the paved area, and opposite the red brick Chapter House, notice behind the railings of the old mason's yard the badly worn head and shoulders of the statue of St Andrew, crisp and new when carved by Bird in 1724 to be mounted on the West Front pediment (**4**). So badly corroded had it

Head of St Andrew.

become by atmospheric weathering, that in 1923 it was replaced and this, the original, was deposited in The Geological Museum in South Kensington as a demonstration of rock weathering. As such, its presence here seems so much more eloquent, and a reminder if we needed one that much more of the original statuary must be in a similar condition requiring a continuing programme of restoration in years to come.

Beyond the Chapter House, which is a Wren building now much restored, the paved area narrows and skirts the southern side of the modern **Paternoster House** (**5**) another unit of the Holford Plan, and, like Juxon House, extensively clad in Portland Stone. At ground floor and first floor levels, however, other stones are involved in the fabric,

Paternoster House.

introducing a measure of contrast in both colour and textures. For example, below the first floor windows, there are polished panels of a silver-grey granite which may be Pelastine Granite from Carnmenellis in Cornwall. A point of interest when looking at this rock from below is the swirling pattern produced by the lath-shaped feldspar crystals, suggestive of fluid movement in the rock melt as it cooled. There is also a hint of local clustering of the same feldspars, producing white cloud-like areas within the rock. In contrast, other panels seem to have dark patches which may be 'heathen' inclusions of the surrounding country rock, or patches of the dark mineral, tourmaline, locally concentrated.

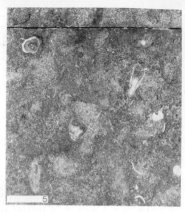

Limestone panel, Paternoster House.

A third rock type in the building comes in the vertical pillars which run from pavement up to first floor level, in the form of dark-toned Carboniferous Limestone, rubbed smooth but unpolished. The rock itself contains areas of colour-contrast in that there are paler-toned, strap-like markings crossing the darker coloured background. This is evidence for trace-fossils within the limestone, indicating that while the sediment was still soft mud, it was burrowed into and digested by mud-eating organisms, which from the size of the tracks here, may have been either bivalves or shrimp-like crustacea. The limestone itself is quite fossiliferous. Its shell fauna includes brachiopods (valves of *Productus* and *Spirifer* seen in cross section), corals (the horn-shaped *Zaphrentites* can be seen cut in several different cross sections, while the colonial *Syringopora* makes up the bushy clumps seen well in the east end entrance) and a great abundance of crinoid debris (the stem ossicles of sea-lilies, scattered over the sea bed after death). These instructive surfaces extend the full length of the building, but are most rewarding in the slabs about the main entrance to the Charterhouse Group offices, where the rock is more fully polished. The fossils mentioned, and the general impression of all the surfaces suggest that the limestone is actually of lower Lower Carboniferous Limestone age (Tournaisian). On this count it could have come either from Belgium and the quarries of the Meuse Valley or from quarries in the west of Ireland.

Within the framework of modern buildings such as Paternoster House, individual shop units can often introduce further varieties of stone through their particular facings. Such is the case with the first of the ground floor units which we neet as we approach from the churchyard, the offices of T.C.B. introduce large surface areas of an attractive cream-coloured stone, with strong evidence of bedding running through the slabs. This stone is Italian Travertine, found widely coutcropping in the hills above Rome. Like stalagmite, it is formed by the deposition of calcium carbonate from groundwater. With most travertines, it is lime chemically precipitated from warm springs emerging on a land surface, and not from cold waters dripping in caves. From its origins, the rock is naturally porous and full of cavities, some of which originate as the lime-sheaths to the stems and roots of aquatic plants. Once again, this is a rock which has valuable non-slip qualities which have caused it to be widely used in paving in the Underground. Here in Paternoster House we see a frequent treatment of the stone, the cavities having been plugged with a cement of equal hardness and then polished smooth to produce Filled- or Stopped-Travertine.

To the east of Paternoster House rises the octagon-shaped modern building, **Bank of Boston House (6)**, involving three further types of stone. First, at ground floor level, there are slabs of 'Black Granite', the rock type already discussed when we met it in Juxon House. This time, however, the rock is not Rustenberg as it is clearly darker and denser through its alteration. It could be from India, Brazil, Morocco or Scan-

Bank of Boston House, New Change.

dinavia. In the circumstances, it is best referred to as being '.. from a Precambrian Shield area of the World', which is its geological context.

The second stone of the building is a dark grey, almost black slate, which once again may be Burlington Slate from the Lake District, but equally could be older Cambrian Slate from North Wales. Some of the panels between the shop fronts are large riven slabs with the rough surface which indicates the gritty character of the original rock. This made it respond poorly to pressure and unable to take the perfect cleavage which is necessary to produce high-quality slate. In another finish, slabs of the same slate have been vertically grooved throughout their total height to produce a scored or corrugated effect. Sadly, it might as well have been plastic or some such artificial material rather than honest stone.

The third and by far the most prominent stone of the Bank, must be the one which occurs in the external walling above street level, which is a white limestone cut in thick cladding slabs. It is a stone which has a slightly blotchy greyness seen from below and at a distance, with a roughness of surface. This rock is the highly fossiliferous variety of Portland Stone, known to the quarrymen as Roach. On account of its fossil content and its cavities, this stone was once passed over by architects who preferred the even-textured Base- or Whit-Bed. The cavernous and rough texture of Roach is caused by the solution of the shell material which made up a large proportion of the original rock. These shells included the famous 'Portland Screw' (the tall spired gastropod, *Procerithium*) and the 'Horses Heads' (the bivalve *Trigonia* which has lost its original shell by solution, leaving an internal filling of the shell space by lime mud, to form an internal cast). As often happens with building stones, some ten years ago, architects seem to have experienced a conversion to the textural possibilities of Roach when introduced into buildings otherwise made up of smooth surfaces. Since then, Roach has quickly gained favour and has been widely used in many City buildings of note in recent years.

Bank of Boston House, detail of surface.

Just to the north of Bank of Boston House, the kiosk at the entrance to **St Paul's Underground Station** (**7**), offers one of the most interesting rock types of the whole area. It is a striking black and white dioritic rock, known to the trade as Tatra 'B' (I am grateful to Alan Nicholson, a keen collector of building stones, for solving what was a problem of identification). As the name suggests, this igneous rock comes from the Tatra Mountain Belt of Czechoslovakia, part of the Hercynian Mountain Chain of central Europe. The rock originally may have had much the same character as the diorite of the West Front steps of St Paul's, but then was altered to such a degree that the igneous rock was transformed into this white-veined, complexly folded and streaked-out metamorphic end product.

At this point, it is worth our while crossing the road intersection at the western end of Cheapside, in order to examine the south wall of **St Vedast-alias Foster** (**8**). This was one of the many City churches rebuilt by Wren after the Great Fire of 1666, and, as was customary, rebuilding involved the use of many tons of good quality Portland Stone. The elegant steeple-crowned tower and the walls facing on to Foster Lane are indeed of good quality, white-weathering stone, but as the wall facing on to the car park of Cheapside House shows, the Portland Stone was merely an outer skin to substantial remnants of the old fab-ric. In this end wall, now freed from the previously screening buildings, we can see irregular sized blocks of flaking Cretaceous Greensand (possibly stone from north Surrey), pale coloured Kentish Rag (Greensand from the Medway Valley), fragments of tile-shaped Roman Brick, as well as flints of all sizes and shapes. All were important elements in the building fabric of pre-Fire London.

Returning now to New Change, the complex of small buildings which now house **St Paul's Choir School** (**9**), offers further examples of Portland Roach but with the advantage that it is now at eye level and accessible for closer study. In the first wall we meet indeed, we see the distinctive cauliflower-shape of a colony of calcareous algae (point 'a' on the accompanying map). Such algae were a constant feature of the Portland environment telling us that the seas were shallow, if not lagoonal, and probably quite warm in temperature. As they are formed of denser and more compact lime, these algae remain unaffected by the waters which dissolved the shell of other organisms and so they remain as solid white masses within the cavernous stone. Interestingly, in the next walls which run at right angles to New Change (point 'b' on the map), it is possible to trace a transition between typical open-textured Roach and the same limestone barely altered by solution. This suggests that the leaching effect has not completely penetrated the lower

St Paul's Choir School from the north.

New Change from the north.

levels of the quarries now being commercially worked on Portland.

The imposing curving fronted building on the opposite side of **New Change** (**10**), is an extension of the Bank of England. In the well established tradition of City buildings, it has a lower course at pavement level of grey-blue granite (possibly Dalbeattie Granite from the Southern Uplands), topped by walls of good quality rubbed red brick with dressings of white Portland Stone. The frame surround to the impressive bronze doors, reintroduces us to Stopped Travertine, a detail repeated in each of the entrances to this building.

The same stone, Stopped Travertine, can be seen again in the ground floor fittings to **The Bank of America** in Watling Street (**11**). This building, known as Gateway House, underwent extensive refurbishing in early 1979 as a result of which pillars, flooring and even the moulded counter surfaces of the Bank are all fashioned in this rich golden stone. This is a fair demonstration of its versatility for either internal or external use. Most of the Travertine of this colour and texture, comes from the very large quarries at Tivoli just outside the City of Rome, and is of very young geological age—Plio-Pleistocene. Travertines of other colours and structures can come from Spain, Portugal, Germany, or Greece.

Where New Change intersects with Cannon Street, stands **Bracken House** the home of The Financial Times (**12**), and a building which offers that rare sight in the City, the use of sandstone as a building material. The greater part of the building is of a warm-toned rough-textured brown brick, but in the lower courses we meet a foundation of rich red stone with slight mottling of paler hue in some places. This is Hollington Stone from the Trias of Staffordshire, the same stone as used by Sir Basil Spence in the rebuilding of Coventry Cathedral in 1956, some two years before the building of Bracken House. It is tempting to think that the architect Sir Albert Richardson considered the pink tone of Hollington Stone in some way appropriate for the headquarters of the Financial Times. The use of this stone, nevertheless, has brought problems. Some blocks and surfaces have clearly suffered from damp, which in turn has produced loss of surface, and some unsightly loss of colour. Seen in bright sunlight, however, from the Queen Victoria Street side, the sandstone positively sparkles as light is reflected from the quartz overgrowths which coat the sand grains. What we also can see quite clearly on the faces of the same blocks, are current-bedding patterns formed when the sand grains were wind-blown sand dunes. As the dunes moved, older structures were planed off and replaced by later structures of the same kind, sweeping forward in great festoon arcs. Such cross-bedding is a means

Bracken House from Queen Victoria St.

of determining the top and bottom of bed units 'fossilised' as sandstones, and happily we can as geologists say that the greater part of Bracken House is right-way-up. As usual, when stone has suffered decay, the patching stands out all-too clearly. It is not easy to match stone. The patch ought to have just the same degree of weathering as the surrounding block in order to blend and harmonise. What is worse, however, is when a 'poultice' of mortar charged with sand grains is packed into a damaged area. Invariably in London the mortar includes tell-tale flint sand which then stands out like a sore thumb on account of its weathering characteristics. In all these points, you can see that our appreciation of a building can be quite different from the normal when we are looking with the eye of the geologist.

Across Distaff Lane to the west, **Scandinavian House** (**13**), offers large surface areas of what is possibly one of the best-known igneous rocks used in ornamental frontages—Larvikite. Here, in the front of the building, slabs show the spectacular blue reflection from the large feldspar crystals which dominate the mineral composition of the rock. Lacking any free silica and hence having no quartz, Larvikite is technically an alkali-syenite rather than a 'granite' (or 'Blue Granite' as it might be

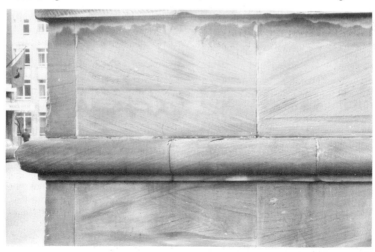

Bracken House, detail of cross-bedding in sandstone.

termed by the Stone Trade). On closer examination, it will be noticed that the larger feldspars are crowded with small opaque grain inclusions which in part may be responsible for the light dispersal which produces the peacock-blue iridescence so distinctive for this rock. Geologically and geographically, Larvikite is almost unique to a small area on the western shores of Oslo Fjord, near the town of Larvik. Quarries in the vicinity have exported the rock for almost a hundred years, providing the familiar polished surfaces of Burton's or Dewhurst's shops which are as much a part of their image as what they sold from inside. Sadly, nowadays, you are as likely to find Larvikite in rough finish (simply saw

might be said that marble is a rock type sometimes very difficult to identify on account of the intergradations of some of the types and because there are several colour tones or venation patterns which recur in different areas.

At this point on the pavement, looking back to New Change, there is good opportunity to take in the effects of the re-structuring of the eastern end of St Paul's Precinct. In the foreground is the paved area of the Festival Garden of 1951, with the steeple of **St Augustine (14)**, once in Watling Street, but now a focal point rising skywards against the horizontal lines of New Change. Immediately behind the steeple are the clustered units of The Choir School. This

West face of Peter's Hill House; columns of Labradorita.

cut and unpolished) or even what is called flame finish, which is in effect a matt surface burned with a thermal lance. You can test this difference of appearance of a familiar rock by looking closely at the slabs which face Distaff Lane. Looking at the surfaces slightly obliquely, you should be able to detect the outline of the large feldspars within the dark groundmass which otherwise has the appearance of concrete. Good natural stone deserves a better treatment, and receives it in the main entrance to Scandinavian House. Here, in this refitted building (1983), we find two contrasting marbles, one the strongly calcite-veined Grigio Fiorito Timau Marble from Udine seen earlier in Juxon House, the other a white marble with a pale yellow streak running through it. It is of unknown source. At this point it

grouping of Roach-clad buildings capped with lead-sheathed overhanging roofs, when seen from this angle, give an aptness to the Pevsner comment that the School gives the impression of, 'a funny hat reminiscent of the morel or some other edible fungus' (Pevsner 1973 p. 203). As planning and architecture, no one could deny that the design and impact of the School are effective.

Peter's Hill House (15), facing directly the South Transept of St Paul's, is another steel-framed building with large areas of glass, but the stone which fills in some of the intervening spaces includes one of the most exotic rock types we shall meet in the course of this walk. The dark pillars which appear to support the entire building are encased in a strikingly metallic blue coloured stone which at first looks a little like the Larvikite which we were looking at in Scandinavian House. It is, however, more blotchy in its blue colouration and studied closely will be seen to have a texture made up of many parallel-aligned colourless crystals which give an appearance akin to tapioca. The rock is one which is variously called by the Trade, Labradorita or Verde Ematita Madreperla, and proves to be a high-grade metamorphic rock, rich in alumina in the form of the mineral cordierite (the colourless tapioca forms). As the Spanish-ness of the name may hint, the rock comes from an area of the High Andes of Argentina, several hundred kilometres to the north of San Juan in the north-west corner of the country. It is a most unusual stone, and is now virtually unobtainable for purely geological reasons.

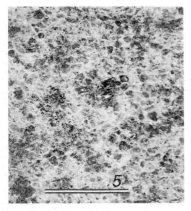

Detail of crystal fabric of Labradorita. Scale in cm.

Other stone in this building includes several types of marble in the foyers and about the lift shafts and stairways. On the east front for example, there are walls of black marble criss-crossed by white calcite veins forming tension-gash patterns clearly highlighted by the dense black background. This is marble which comes from the Ardennes of Belgium, known variously as Noire Vein or Bleu Belge (a name which is difficult to understand on account of the colour of the stone). The rock is of Carboniferous age, and from country which underwent considerable deformation at the same time that South West England was being shaped into the cliff forms of Devon and Cornwall. Pale grey-streaked marble (?Italian Dove Marble) has been split and laid out in matching patterns up the staircases of the west front of the building.

Continuing westwards along St Paul's Churchyard, back to our starting point, the curving front of the Edwardian building **Condor House (16)**, offers sight of two contrasting Scottish granites in the tall pilasters which front the building. One is the dark grey stone from the excessively deep quarry within the city limits of Aberdeen, Rubislaw Granite, a stone characterised by its slightly foliated (layered) texture, as well as the wealth of small, dark inclusions of country rock (the xenoliths or 'heathen' of earlier discussion). The second rock is Peterhead Granite, a much more even-grained rock with a very distinctive salmon-pink coloured orthoclase feldspar making up much of the rock. Peterhead Granite also shows xenoliths, some of them distinctly black and recognisable as pieces of Highland schist caught up within the molten granite. Others which are of greater interest are those which are much paler in tone, indicating a change brought about by the growth within the fragment of the same pink orthoclase feldspars which dominate the granite proper. Once again, as in the case of the Shap bollards discussed earlier, this seems to prove the molten and assimilating character of granites in the crust.

A short detour down Dean's Court, offers us further large surface areas of polished Larvikite to study in the walls of **No. 4 St Paul's Churchyard (17)**. This office block is of cleaned Portland Stone, but the entire ground floor frontage is faced with substantial blocks of the two contrasting types of the blue Norwegian stone, one the almost black Pearl Larvikite, the other the paler blue Emerald Pearl Larvikite. Edwardian and older Larvikite in buildings seems mostly the dark sombre variety, whereas modern buildings in the City invariably seem to be of the electric-blue type. Perhaps age, or depth within the quarried layers have something to do with this. So we complete our round trip back to the statue of Queen Anne, still steadfastly looking down Ludgate Hill, which happens to be the course of our second walk.

West Front steps, St Paul's

Ludgate Hill and Fleet Street from St Paul's

LUDGATE HILL TO
QUEEN VICTORIA STREET

From Queen Anne's statue it is worth looking at the details of **No. 4 St Paul's Churchyard** (**1**, and the last stop of the previous walk) to take in its architectural style. We can also note the effects of surface cleaning of the Portland Stone. Like many offices of the Edwardian period, there is an ebullience about No. 4 with its combination and confusion of all the classical orders, seen when we scan the front from pavement to roof level. It is as if the architect felt obliged to reflect the detail of the West Front opposite, and then to go one better with a few Baroque touches added for good measure. At this time, there was no 'cladding' approach when using Portland Stone; the walls are of solid blocks of the natural stone, but for all that, there has been some loss of surface here as a result of cleaning involving sand-blasting techniques. Under such bombardment by quartz grains (hardness 7), limestones (hardness 3) can become pock-marked so that their surfaces look more like those of sandstones at first glance. Cleaners are less drastic these days, but it has taken several years for some lessons to be learnt in the treatment of stonework which a geologists would have regarded as self-evident.

The adjoining building, **Nos. 1–3 St Paul's Churchyard** (**2**), currently Abbey Life House, has details similar to those of Condor House (stop **16** of the first walk). Here, however, the grey granite forming the base to the pilasters is Bessbrook Granite from the Armagh district of Ulster rather than the grey Rubislaw Granite of the previous building. The distinction between these two granites lies in the grey-brown colour of the Irish granite, and the compact white feldspar crystals which are evenly distributed throughout it as a rock. Rubislaw is darker and more even grained in texture.

At the top of Ludgate Hill, on the north side, the modern shop fronts (**3**) display semi-polished slabs of brown Nabresina Limestone. This rock, crowded with finely fragmented shell debris, giving it a characteristic oatmeal texture, is from the Cretaceous of Istria at the northern end of the Adriatic, close to Trieste. In the centre of the same block unit, the office of **The Colonial Mutual Insurance Company** (**4**), offers a strongly contrasting British marble in the dark-toned Torquay or Ashburton Marble from South Devon. Whether on the slightly dulled surfaces of the external walling or the fully polished slabs within the office foyer it is not difficult to find good examples of the fossils which prove

Statue of Queen Anne (Italian Marble) backed by the offices of St Paul's Churchyard.

its Devonian age. These include large calcitic hemispheres which are the colonial coelenterate *Stromatopora*, the more truly coral-like forms of *Favosites* and *Heliolites*, and the branching stems of *Pachypora*. The dark groundmass is dotted with shell fragments of brachiopods and accumulations of crinoid ossicles. Evidence that the limestone underwent a measure of deformation as well as recrystallisation, can be detected from the distorted oval shapes of the normally round sectioned crinoid ossicles, and from the rupture and veining of well-defined shapes such as coral corallites. The reddening of the rock, along veins or joint planes, is attributed to the percolation of iron minerals from the later cover of New Red Sandstone which formerly spread across the whole area of the marble quarries from Torquay and Paignton and beyond. Unlike Nabresina which is often termed a 'marble' although it has not undergone any measure of heat or pressure, Torquay or Ashburton Marble is a true marble in the sense understood by geologists, being one of the products of the folding which affected the whole of South West England during the Hercynian Orogeny.

Beyond Stationer's Hall Court, the columns and arches of Nos. 30–32 Ludgate Hill, **The Burnley Building Society (5)**, are of blood-red Scandinavian Granite, either Swedish Imperial Red or Balmoral Granite. Both

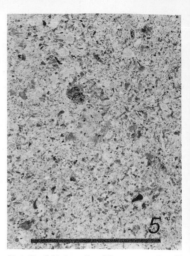

Detail of Nabresina Limestone in pillars to The Colonial Mutual Insurance Company, 24, Ludgate Hill. Scale in cm.

are deeper in tone than most British red granites, and for their richer colour, became popular in late Victorian times when they acquired their patriotic names as a further guarantee of entry. Some Scandinavian rocks at that time, when we still had a flourishing granite trade in areas such as Aberdeenshire, were cut and polished in this country as an additional recommendation. Geologically, most of the Swedish and Finnish rocks of this nature are older granites of the late-Precambrian, and

Detail of Torquay Marble, The Colonial Mutual Insurance Company 24, Ludgate Hill.

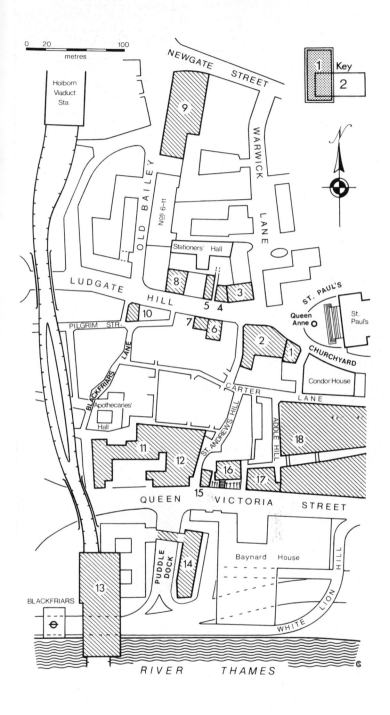

The church of **St Martin's-within-Ludgate** (**8**), midway down the hill on the north side, is another Wren church rebuilt after the Great Fire of 1666. It is now so confined by other buildings that only the square tower faces on to the street. This tower, capped by a very impressive steeple, was cased in white-weathering Portland Stone, but at pavement level, some of the rougher-surfaced original masonry, including flaking Greensand, can be seen. This casing of older masonry by new stone is something we have already seen in the walls of St Vedast, Foster Lane (Stop **8** of walk 1).

Dark red Swedish Granite, paler, grey Cornish Granite, The Burnley Building Society, Ludgate Hill.

may have been modified by later earth movements of Caledonian date (the folding of the Grampian Highlands was of this period). For this reason, some of the polished surfaces show that the feldspar crystals have been crushed and are shot through with shear planes caused by movement under stress. Other rocks are decidedly gneissic, their minerals being drawn out into recognisable streaks which seemingly wrap around less disturbed cores or 'augen'. In all these respects, Scandinavian red granites are both colourful and instructive when we meet them in the street.

As if to counterbalance this show of Scandinavian rock types, the buildings on the opposite, south side of Ludgate Hill, from **No. 19** to the grand arch to Ludgate Square (**6**), are fronted by columns of pinkish-brown Shap Granite. This is readily comparable with the bollards of the pavement in front of St Paul's, and is identified by the common occurrence of the large pink orthoclase feldspar crystals in both. Swedish granite returns in the entrance to **Lloyd's Bank** (**7**) in the form of the distinctive Virgo Granite. This is another red granite, but one in which stresses suffered by the quartz crystals have produced blue or violet colours as light is internally reflected. These structurally deformed 'blue quartz' granites' come mainly from the south of Sweden, including localities close to the Baltic Coast:

Ludgate Hill including St Martin's within Ludgate.

From Ludgate Hill, a detour to the north along Old Bailey, takes us past some typical late-Victorian offices (Nos. 6, 7–10) with some ornate details in granite and terracotta, before we come to the new extension to the **Central Criminal Court** (The Old Bailey by its more familiar name) (**9**). When the new building was completed in 1973, opinion was divided over the contrast between the smooth ashlar finish and strong verticals of the modern extension, and the massive Baroque detail of the 1902 building (by E. W. Mountford). However, the extension is undoubtedly impressive and imposing in its own terms. The stone of the main external walls is high quality Portland Whit Bed, rubbed to a smooth surface finish, and so

Central Criminal Court, Old Bailey. Merrivale Granite to 2m; Portland Whit Bed above.

closely jointed as to give the impression of a solid shell overall. At pavement level, the lower courses and the arches are of hammer dressed grey Merrivale Granite from quarries on the west side of Dartmoor. In spite of the rough-dressed finish, large porphyritic feldspar crystals which are randomly distributed throughout the rock can be picked out on closer examination of the walls. Only visitors to the Central Criminal Courts themselves have the opportunity to study two distinct varieties of Italian travertine from the Tivoli quarries near Rome, which are used for the interior walling, flooring, and staircase surfaces.

Back to Ludgate Hill, the **Midland Bank (10)**, built in 1891 by the architect T. H. Colcutt, and recently cleaned, shows grey hammer dressed granite (probably Cornish) up to first floor levels, and terracotta above. Terracotta was a favourite material of Victorian architects, because it could be moulded to produce decorative detail for buildings at minimal cost. It also has durability beyond that of most stone, and even the best quality brick. Terracotta was made from high-alumina clays from the Coal Measures of the Midland counties in England, the clays ground very finely to produce a clay paste, and then fired in kilns to a high temperature. In this process, it acquired its hard surface, unchanged by normal weathering agencies.

Behind the Bank, Blackfriars Lane twists downhill towards the river through an area of war-time demolition and emerging older buildings (the **Apothecaries Hall** for instance). Geologically, its best offerings are the large surface areas of street cobbles and kerbstones A wide range of igneous and metamorphic rocks is present, from granites (red Mountsorrel Granite from Charnwood Forest; grey Cornish Granite; red granite with prominent white feldspars from Sweden) to dolerite and basalt (dense blue-grey rocks probably from the west Midlands or Scotland) and a wide variety of gneisses (mostly from Scandinavia). It is worth remembering that the colourful mosaic which survives here, challenging our powers of recognition, was once the pattern for all the streets and lanes of the City.

Following the lane past The Apothecaries Hall and the railway viaduct approach to Blackfriars Station, the ground opens out into the reconstructed Printing House Square, occupied mainly by the overlapping L-shaped blocks which were once the headquarters of 'The Times' (**11**). The buildings, designed by Llewellyn-Davies & Partners in 1960, are of interest to us in that the upper floors are separated by large panels of green Lake District Slate, rubbed to a smooth, satiny finish. This is a rock which is a fine-grained, water-lain volcanic ash of the Ordovician Borrowdale Volcanic Series. As such, it can show a wide diversity of sedimentary structures which commonly occur in soft wet sediment. These include slump-bedding, erosional channels, flake-pebble con-

The Continental Bank, Printing House Square. Slabs of pale Lake District Slate, showing sedimentary structures.

glomerate, and graded-bedding, all clearly seen on these cleavage slabs because of the striking colour contrasts which are present. Rocks of this particular colour are found in the quarries of the Langdale Valley or the Kirkstone Pass of the Lake District central belt. Here, the whole succession of the Borrowdale Volcanic Series has been subjected to stresses during folding which have produced the strong cleavage of these ashes. In the old 'Times' building, these rock panels can only be seen at a distance in what is now the premises of **The Continental Bank** (of America). Large surface areas of the slates are to be seen, however, at street level in the south wall of **'The Observer'** building, where the structures mentioned can be studied at leisure (**12**). A very durable material, the only defect in the slate as a facing stone is a tendency to lose some of its original colour with the passage of years, but treatment can be given which can refresh the

Detail of Lake District Slate, The Observer building, St Andrew's Hill. Graded bedding; ripple-mark.

surfaces, preventing the 'washed-out' look seen in some buildings.

Blackfriars Station (**13**) was largely reconstructed during the 1970's, when the new building facing on to Queen Victoria Street was surfaced with the handsome reddish-brown granite, Imperial Mahogany, imported from Dakota, U.S.A. This, and similar granites from Quebec have become very fashionable with architects at the present time. All are what are often referred to as 'older granites', meaning that they have been involved after their formation in later mountain building events. Quite simply, this later history is responsible for the streaking out of their minerals into bands, and introduces a mild foliation into the rock—a structure often associated with metamorphic rock types. A further feature may be the crushing of the large, well-formed feldspars, as well as a tendency for them to be bunched together into lenses (the 'augen' of German descriptive accounts). Many of the panels of the frontage of Blackfriars Station offer beautiful examples of these part-metamorphic features of what technically might be called 'Gneiss' rather than 'Granite'.

Another granite, this time without any shadow of doubt as to its igneous character, occurs in the bridging structure which crosses Puddle Dock to link up with the **Mermaid Theatre** (**14**). This whole building complex is faced with a beautiful pale grey granite, which contrasts in colour strongly with the

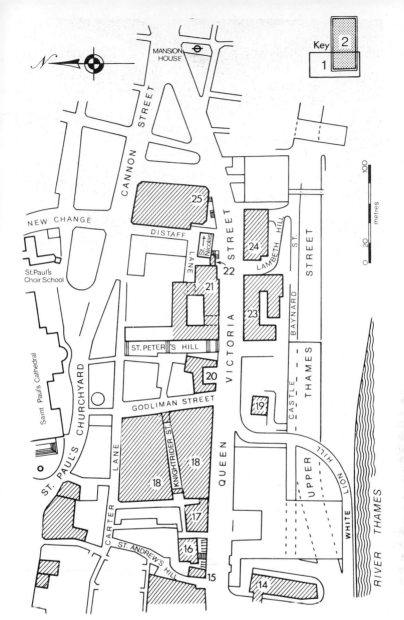

nearby Dakota Imperial Mahogany. Seen at close quarters, the texture of this grey granite is a random mosaic of grey glassy quartz, combined with white microperthitic feldspar, and large patches of green-tinged, partly kaolinitised orthoclase feldspar. Black biotite mica is liberally scattered through the rock to darken its otherwise pale colour. Not only is this an attractive rock which catches the sunlight in a splendid way, but it also introduces us to another source of imported stone to our ever-growing catalogue—this time Italy. To the trade, this granite is known as Montorfano, and is one of several silver-grey granites of late-Carboniferous age currently available from the Southern Alps, Sardinia, parts of Spain and Portugal. This particular Montorfano Granite can be recognised from its pale green colour cast, arising from the altered orthoclase feldspar minerals. Geologically, Montorfano is a northern extension of the well-known Baveno Granite massif, outcropping on the western shores of Lake Maggiore.

View eastwards up Queen Victoria Street. Foreground left, 'The Observer' building; middle distance, Bible House and Faraday House.

Our walk now follows the line of Queen Victoria Street, climbing due east from near-river level at Blackfriars to the level of the Taplow Terrace, some 22 m higher, on which St Paul's Cathedral stands. The street with its direct alignment, was a major piece of town planning of the years 1867–71, when its course was driven through a chaos of old buildings and lanes which clustered downslope from the Cathedral. At the same time, the District Line was being tunnelled into the same hillslope, with chimney vents to allow the escape of smoke from the steam engines originally used. This smoke undoubtedly contributed to the begriming of the church of St Nicolas-Cole-Abbey, and several of the brand new offices which were put up along the line of the street. The street has seen many changes through War damage, and more recently through the modernisation of the Embankment roadways, particularly on the south side, where new buildings now alternate with open spaces. Most of the geological interest centres upon buildings which survive on the north side of the road.

At the foot of St Andrew's Hill, the public house **The Baynards Castle** (**15**) has frontage columns of pink Peterhead Granite set off as often seems to have been the case, with bases of contrasting dark grey Rubislaw Granite. The upper floors are of a fiery red terracotta. The Wren church of **St Andrew-by-the-Wardrobe**

(**16**), combines darkly-weathered red brick with Portland Stone dressings, and clearly has suffered from several partial destructions and restorations. It now presents an interesting study for several stonework problems. Some of the Portland Stone, for example, has blistered and flaked—a fault well-seen in the gateposts at street level. As the inscription records, these particular pillars were restored in 1901 in honour of the well-known architectural historian, Bannister Fletcher, one-time Churchwarden of St Andrews. No better

Gatepost to St Andrew by the Wardrobe. Blistered and broken surfaced Portland Stone.

Close-up of the dedication tablet of 1901; crazed sulphate surface skin to Portland Stone.

fate has befallen the York Stone of the steps rising steeply to the main entrance, which show flaking of surface (a consequence of dampness and frosting) as well as considerable tread-wear which has been repaired in a piece-meal fashion. In fact, everywhere in these stone details, 'dental repairs' simply serve to draw attention to the decay, as new stone stands out clearly against the older fabric. In the case of the dark paste used to repair the Portland Stone blisters, the match could not have been worse as there are no dark, flinty grains in the original stone. In all this, while the immediate aim may have been to arrest decay, the visual effect is rather disastrous.

Beyond the church, **Bible House** (**17**), the headquarters of the British and Foreign Bible Society, opened by its President, Lord Shaftesbury, in 1867, offers several rock types which may already be familiar to you. The building itself is an Italian 'palazzo' in its design, rising from massive slabs of granite at street level. This last rock is dark grey in colour and rough-riven in its finish, although the surfaces are further roughened by flaking which results from rising damp and salt penetration from the local groundwater. From its dark colour, however, and the presence of dark schist xenoliths, it seems certain that this is Rubislaw Granite from the quarries which once worked within the city limits of Aberdeen. In the entrance to the building, there are polished columns of Peterhead

Granite, offering the usual colour contrast to Rubislaw's sombre tone. The upper walls of Bible House are of yellowed Portland Stone, slightly pock-marked from recent cleaning. In spite of this, the surfaces are worth looking at for the naturalistic flowers and grasses which were lightly carved on the face of the building as a part of its decoration. The building was designed by the architect I'Anson, who otherwise was responsible for several 'Gothic' offices and banks in the City.

Faraday Building (**18**), put up in 1932 for the G.P.O. Telecommunications Division, continues the combination of a granite base, topped by upper floors in Portland Stone—a pattern which we see in many commercial buildings. Here, the Portland Stone is of a whiteness matching that of Shell-Mex House on the Embankment, or Senate House in Bloomsbury. When it was completed, Faraday House was strongly criticised, partly on account of its monolithic form, but principally because its nine storeys blotted out views of St Paul's from the river. In 1975, as other buildings were cleared from the street, the suggestion was made that the upper floors might be removed in an attempt to open up the vista from Thameside. Today, although most of its telecommunications work is transferred to Baynards House opposite, Faraday Building remains a white monolith of Portland Stone, overtopping all surrounding structures. Otherwise, building clearance locally to allow for road improvement has had some good effect. For example, it has revealed the neat, compact character of the Wren church of **St Benet's Paul's Wharf** (**19**), once completely hemmed-in by tall buildings, but now standing clear and prominent to the south of the street.

On the north side, further east, **The College of Arms** (**20**), headquarters of The College of Heralds, is of old, deep-red 17th century bricks, set off by Portland Stone dressings to the stairs and balustrades. The building itself dates from 1688, but the railings closing the quadrangle and based upon patched blocks of Old Red Sandstone, are of later date. The same gates and railings were transferred here from Goodrich Court, Hereford (Pevsner, 1962), and it is on the strength of this information that the red sandstone is judged to be Old—rather than New Red Sandstone—a distinction normally very difficult to make purely upon appearances or colour alone. The forecourt of the College is yet another area of diverse and interesting cobble stones of a wide range of igneous rock types.

Nos. 122–128 Queen Victoria Street (**21**), complete the office complex of Peter's Hill (see Stop **15** of the first walk), extending St Paul's Churchyard downslope. Seen from Peter's Hill Steps, the buildings show tall panels of dark grey Burlington Slate from quarries overlooking the Duddon Estuary in the southern Lake District. In these riven cleavage slabs, the colour banding which can be faintly detected on the rough surface, is a trace of the true bedding of the Silurian age sediment. Being of coarser grain, this rock is not so well-cleaved as the green Lake District Slate seen earlier in 'The Observer' walls. At first floor levels in the same building, there are panels of smooth-rubbed grey granite of unknown provenance. The rock is fine grained, without any race of a porphyritic texture; with its blue-grey colour, it is possible that it is a Southern Uplands granite such as Dalbeattie from Kircudbrightshire. Where Distaff Lane passes beneath this building to join Queen Victoria Street, the supporting columns are faced with the strikingly blue metamorphic rock, Labradorita (see Stop **15** of walk 1). Here it is seen to better advantage because, with their south facing aspect, the columns catch afternoon sunlight which can pick up the slightly translucent quality of this cordierite rock. Within the framework of the offices, there are several entrances and stairways fitted out with other ornamental stones. The west wall and surround to No. 128 for example, are lined with the distinctive, limpid marble, White Crystal (∗), a rock which shows evidence of the complete recrystallisation of the original calcite so that the marble is now a mosaic of large crystals of the same mineral. The back wall of the same foyer is of polished slabs of pale buff marble, with well-marked bands of brown bivalvian shells. The rock is an Italian limestone, either Perlato or Repen Zola. Both are slightly recrystallised limestones, in which pressure-solution effects give rise to the darker stylolite lines within the rock. Neither are true 'marbles' in the sense of the term as used by geologists, requiring alteration by heat and pressure. By contrast, the flooring is of pure white Statuary Marble, which, like White Crystal, satisfies all such geological criteria. When we look at the external walling to No. 124, we see again green Lake District Slate, the volcanic ash from the Borrowdale Volcanic Series previously seen in 'The Observer' building. Here, the slate is rough-riven, but once again, the sedimentary bedding is picked out by colour contrasts running across the slabs.

Further east and up the slope of the street, the low building (**22**) extending from the tall block we have just examined (all the premises of Deloitte, Haskins & Sells), offers us extensive surfaces of Portland Roach. Here, in the low walls and steps, it is rich in specimens of the 'Portland Screw' (high-spired gastropods) as well as the cauliflower-like growths of calcareous algae seen in the walls of St Paul's Choir School, New Change. The slabs here deserve close study to gain some idea of the rich range of Upper Jurassic shell fauna present in Portland Stone. Such study can be made on the steps or in the garden area between the street and Distaff Lane, out of the way of traffic and pedestrian flow on the busy pavement.

On the opposite side of the street, the headquarters building of **The Salvation Army** (**23**), is of buff coloured brick, with Portland Stone dressings. As is often the case with modern buildings of essentially simple design and materials, touches of

Nos. 114–116 Queen Victoria Street. Combination of Portland Roach (dark, mottled) and Portland Whit Bed (pale).

more decorative stone are introduced into the entrance and foyer areas. In this case, there is extensive use of dense black, polished igneous rock of the type referred to commonly as 'black granite'. Once again, the precise geographical origin is uncertain, and clearly, the character of the original rock was later altered by the introduction of metallic ores and weathering products of ferromagnesian minerals. Outwardly, the rock is of the type often called Ebony Black, or Nubian Black, and is very much denser and more uniform than the South African 'black granite' met earlier in these walks. By contrast,

one wall of the foyer, and the dedication tablet, are of the brown Cretaceous Nabresina Limestone, from the hills above Trieste in the northern Adriatic.

Beyond Lambeth Hill, **Walker House (24)** on the same side of the street, is likewise interesting for the touches of marble which we can find in an otherwise ordinary building. At the western end, the entrance and staircase of the London-American Group of Companies, No. 95, Queen Victoria Street, are lined with a beautiful pale cream marble, crowded with the cross sections of rudistid bivalves, distinctive for their thick shell-walls. Rudists flourished as oyster-bank communities of shells in warm, lime-rich seas. In a time sense, they clearly indicate that this rock's origin was somewhere in a Cretaceous succession of a Mediterranean country (Spain, Southern France, or Italy). Rudists are unique bivalves, usually with one valve strongly conical, and resembling a robust coral. This resemblance, however, immediately breaks down when we see that there is a second valve, smaller, and lid-like to the cone-shaped valve. The thick, darker-coloured sections through these shells provide the attractive 'figure' to this marble. The same marble occurs in the internal walls of No. 87, at the other end of the range of buildings, closest to Mansion House Station. In between, the entrance and walls of the **Midland Bank,** offer large surface areas of Italian Grigio Fiorito Timau Marble, a grey rock, criss-crossed with strong and prominent veins of white calcite. The rock is of Devonian age, although fossils to prove this point are not easy to recognise in the altered state of the limestone.

At this point, our walk has brought us close to the south face of **Bracken House** (**25**, also Stop **12** of the first walk), with its rich red sandstone walls facing on to Queen Victoria Street. The short flight of steps to the street, and the walls which surround the paved area at a higher level, offer some splendid examples of current-bedding in the sandstone blocks. With the advantage of the southern aspect, the surfaces catch whatever sunlight there is and reflect it from the quartz crystal surfaces which have grown upon the original sand grains. As mentioned on the previous occasion (Stop **12**, walk one), this is Red Hollington Stone from Staffordshire. From this point, the walker can easily reach the Underground stations of Mansion House, or Bank, passing buildings which are the subject for other geological walks (Cheapside, and Cannon Street).

Choir School & Festival Gardens

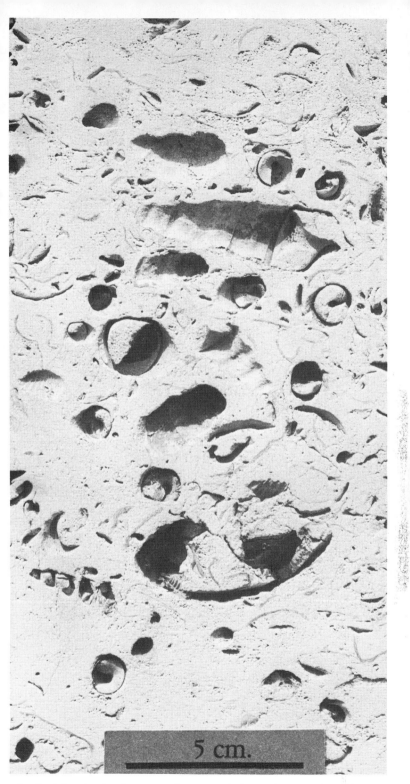

Portland Roach, showing casts of gastropods (cone-shapes and round cross-sections) and bivalves (the curving and bracket shaped outlines).

St Augustine's steeple and Watling Street from the dome of St Paul's.

CHEAPSIDE AND GUILDHALL

For this walk, we start in New Change, in what was the latter third of our first walk, but this time we deliberately turn our back upon St Paul's with its predictable geology of Portland Stone. Instead, we set out down Watling Street through a section of the City in which it is difficult to describe fixed points for others to follow, such are the changes which can take place within the space of months. Watling Street was a Victorian commercial street, built upon a foundation course which was a mediaeval lane framed by close-spaced houses. The warehouses, chambers and offices built in the 19th century fossilised the original pattern. Now in 1984, it is an area where redevelopment of small sites into larger units more suitable for present day uses comes into conflict with its designation as a Conservation Area of the City. This status was well-defined as 'an area of close-knit buildings, set out along the lines of old lanes leading to Thameside from the higher ground of Cornhill, crossed by others leading from Ludgate to The Tower' (Lloyd, 1976). Across this tight pattern, Victorian road improvements cut broad swathes in the shape of Queen Street, from the Thames to Guildhall (1836), and Queen Victoria Street, from Blackfriars to Bank (1867–71). These cuts created the many diamond- or wedge-shaped sites which cluster in the vicinity of Mansion House and the end of Cannon Street. When rebuilding occurred in the 19th century, architects accepted both the irregular ground plan of sites, and the confined space, as they crystallised their buildings to a unified general height and style, and gave a new unity to the area. To some extent, this unity is what is at risk in 1984, as the fabric of Victorial buildings has decayed and requires either renovation or replacement. The general scale could so easily be ignored by piecemeal growth of glass giants set in the midst of surviving offices and chambers. Equally at risk, and just as much a part of the Conservation Area concern, are the skylines and the prospect of well-known landmarks such as St Paul's from long acknowledged viewpoints such as Watling Street.

Interpose one out-of-scale modern building into this frame, and the damage could be irreparable. It is of course difficult to reconcile everyone's hopes in this debate, including those who rightly wish to see architects today given the opportunity to add good modern buildings to the classic 'townscape' of the City. All one can ask is that nothing is done without due deliberation and discussion of what might be at risk.

There is little to say about the west end of Watling Street beyond what has already been said in Walk 1, except perhaps to enthuse over the stopped travertine of The Bank of America on the right hand side of the street. At the crossing with Bread Lane, the southern extension of **Bow Bells House (1)** is of the same period (1958–60) and not very exciting in its architecture. Geologically, however, it does offer at pavement level, panels of 'black granite' which are worth examining as they often catch the afternoon sun to good effect. As has already been said about this rock type, it is not strictly a granite, being without the mineral quartz in its makeup, rather it is a rock type which should be called gabbro, and then be recognised as having suffered considerable alteration. Usually, all the original minerals have become crowded with inclusions of grains of metallic ores, giving the rock a dense and dark cast when polished. Seen here in Bow Bells House, the original minerals are identified by outlines of bronze-lustred pyrite, giving the black rock a rich reflecting surface (when clean). It is highly probable that the gabbro came from South Africa, and would probably have a trade name such as Ebony Black as a consequence. In contrast, the Watling Street face of this same building shows a brilliant white Portland Stone cladding. Several of the slabs are crossed by very rich shell bands, and in the space of twenty five years of exposure, the harder shell fragments, mainly of Jurassic oysters, have emerged from the originally flat-dressed surfaces as the softer limestone matrix has been eaten back by rainwash and corrosion.

At this point, Watling Street narrows down to its Conservation Area

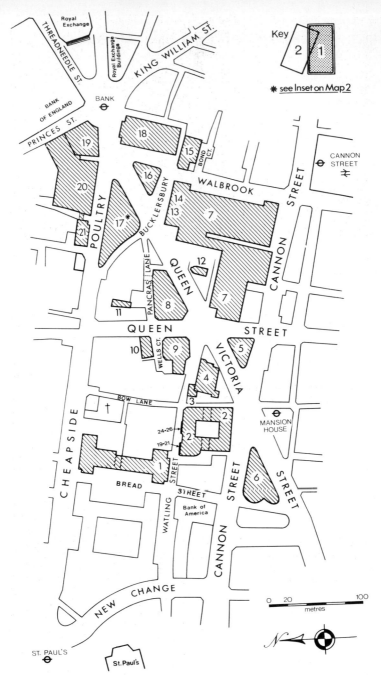

character and we see the ware-houses which were picked out for special mention during European Architectural Heritage Year (Crawford, 1976). Built of brick with stone dressings of Middle Jurassic lime-stones these buildings were almost demolished to make way for the new Midland Bank complex fronting on to Cannon Street. Happily, they now survive, integrated into the structure of the Bank and with all their special features emphasised by cleaning and new paint, as much as new use for their space. **Nos. 23–24** for example are now the bar 'The Pavilion End' (**2**). The newer parts of the building involve large surface areas of buff coloured stopped travertine, surfaces which show all

Credit Lyonnais Bank from Cannon Street junction; dark areas are of Nubian Black Gabbro.

the features of this well-bedded lime deposit formed by strong spring emissions during relatively young geological time periods.

Back in Watling Street, almost at its junction with Queen Street, the premises **Nos. 30–32**, formerly The Banco de Santander (**3**), offers another 'black granite' at pavement level, neatly contrasting with white Portland Stone facings at higher level. It is worthwhile comparing this fairly recent example of Portland Stone with the same rock type in the north wall of **St Mary Aldermary** next door (**4**). The 17th century stone has become deeply pitted and dissolved on flatter surfaces, while in damper corners away from the sun, the rock has blistered and broken from repeated wetting and drying, and frosting over the years. As usual, there have been attempts to patch and restore the damaged areas—the lost corners and broken blisters—but often with results that are too conspicuous to improve the situation let alone disguise the original defect. As well as furnishing these details of fabric, the point we have now reached is one of those strategic viewpoints in the City from which to survey the changing architectural and geological styles of the past century, so let us look around.

Directly opposite us is the ornate mass of **Albert Buildings** (**5**), built in 1871 by the architect F. J. Ward, with nothing very much to offer geologically, but everything that is eye-catching in its Italianate detail at all floor levels. Principally of brick and stucco, overpainted battleship grey, Albert Buildings figures in our Cannon Street walk (walk four), as does its modern counterpart to the west, the equally wedge-shaped **Credit Lyonnais Bank** at the top of Queen Victoria Street (**6**). The one is High Victorian Gothic, and ornate; the other very Modern and clean-lined. Looking east across Queen Street, we see the western end of **Bucklersbury House** (**7**), a building of the late-fifties, with a thin skin of Portland Stone, set off in colour by bands

Aldermary House from Queen Street; foreground left, Albert Buildings with elaborate details in stucco.

of ceramic tile in its upper floors, and substantial courses of pale blue Larvikite at pavement level (again, this building is explored more fully in the Cannon Street walk). Having identified a pattern typical for the 1950's, it is interesting to turn to the other corner of the Queen Street-Queen Victoria Street junction, and take in the form of **Lloyds Bank (8)**, built in the earlier fifties as The Bank of London and South America. Here we have solid walls of massive blocks of good quality Portland Stone, the Bank emerging with the whiteness of other substantial monuments of Empire after some thirty years of weathering. Small details such as the steer's heads, the sombreros and the draped ponchos of the keystones to the window arches—all identifying the association with South America—survive as slightly skittish jokes in an otherwise deadly serious building. As is customary for City banks, there is a base course to the whole which is a grey-blue fine grained granite (?Dalbeattie, or one of the Southern Uplands granodiorites) not easy to pinpoint in this surface finish,. There are also touches of travertine about the entrance at the corner.

Turning now to the building closest to us, we come to **Aldermary House (9)**, a tower of natural stone with windows less prominent than is often the case in modern buildings. The grey stone at pavement level and extending into the verticals at the corner of the tower is a medium-grained grey granite, with a high proportion of dark minerals, including biotite mica and hornblende. The texture is finer than that seen in most Cornish granites seen so far. The rock is in fact Creetown Granite from Kirkcudbrightshire, one of the options which we were considering a moment ago for the granite of Lloyds Bank opposite. In the door surrounds to the Watling Street entrance, and the main entrance from Queen Street, we see grey-black Rustenberg Bon Accord Gabbro from the Bushveld Complex of South Africa, its dark tone effectively setting off the paler Creetown panels. Looking at the pale-coloured stone of the greater part of the upper floors, it would be easy to say 'Portland Stone', such is the dominance of that rock in the City all around us. But not so here. From across Watling Street, if you look closely in oblique light at the panels

Aldermary House from Queen Victoria Street; walls of Pentelic Marble, the darker base of Dalbeattie Granite.

about the windows, you should be able to detect a 'grain' running across the slabs where they have weathered. This reveals that the stone in question is a white marble, not polished as it would be for internal use, but left with a matt surface. Nowhere can you see any trace of shells emerging as the stone weathers back, in the way which would characterise any grade of Portland Stone. Other details to Aldermary House, the headquarters of The Fire Protection Association, include facings of a dark red Swedish granite in the low walls at pavement level. There are also large expanses of polished marble in the entrance foyer and in the pillars to the mezzanine floor, involving white Pentelic Marble from Greece, and the strongly veined Grey Calacatta Marble from Italy.

Beyond Aldermary House is the cùl-de-sac of Wells Court, lined on its two sides by Victorian commercial offices. The block closest to Queen Street is now a restaurant and bar, **The Golden Fleece (10)**, with strongly coloured red-rendered pillars very prominent against the upper floors. Some years ago, these were visibly of poorly weathered New Red Sandstone—a problem which has been solved by the present rendering. In the same renovation, the formerly begrimed stonework of the upper floors has been cleaned and now stands as very characteristic Bath Stone, even-toned orange-brown in colour, and equally even-grained and without any strongly bedded character detectable.

Crossing Queen Street to Pancras Lane, tucked away behind the re-faced Girard Bank, lies **No. 12 Pancras Lane**. This 'chambers' of 1899, is an interesting building of yellow stock brick, with stone dressings of Portland Stone, still occupied by legal firms (**11**). Standing back from the Lane and the created open space with its planted trees this building, with its massive door-surround and carved scallop shells, adds a welcome touch to local 'townscape'. Pancras Lane leads us back to the traffic of Queen Victoria Street, on the other side of which lies a less-peaceful stopping point for our excursion. This is the reconstructed ground-plan of the **Mithraic Temple** (**12**), transferred to the front of Bucklersbury House from the banks of the Walbrook where it was discovered in the course of excavations for foundations in 1954. Such was the interest at the time that Dr Grimes of the London Museum was given the opportunity to excavate the structure in full, with some of the first public viewing platforms on City sites, before reconstructing this ground plan in space set aside for the purpose on Queen Victoria Street. Not everyone would agree that this was appropriate. A Mithraeum was in all likelihood a dark, ill-lit subterranean cave, not something to be exposed to the light of day. As geologists, however, we have to be grateful for the token record of the stone which was employed. Much of it was rough-dressed blocks of cream-coloured Kentish Rag, used elsewhere as the principal wall stone of Roman *Londinium*, and here as low walling and the rounded bases of columns which supported the roof. Otherwise in the structure we can pick out the flat tile-shaped Roman Bricks, levelling up the wall-courses at intervals, and the irregular shaped flints which fill the space between the dressed stones.

Behind the platform on which the Mithraeum stands, the Temple Court wing of Bucklersbury House, offers only panels of stopped travertine in the entrance to The Sumitomo Bank, and the offices of The Legal & General Insurance Company. Both premises are fronted by broad paved areas of York Stone, from the Coal Measures of the West Yorkshire Coalfield. Variety increases, however, when we move to the walling of the Italian restaurant, and the combined premises of **The Scottish-** and **The Norwich Union Insurance Companies** (**13**), which are clad in brilliant pale-blue Larvikite which faces whatever sunlight there may be in the afternoons. Such light is needed to pick out the grains of ore minerals which zone the large feldspar crystals, and produce the overall iridescence of the whole surface. Equally elegant is the stonework which we can see in the entrance foyer to the **Scottish Union Office** (**14**). Here, the back wall is of white-veined green serpentinite. The door itself is framed by panels of the Belgian black marble, criss-crossed by tension-gash veins, which is, rather oddly, called Bleu Belge Marble (it isn't blue at all, but black by anyone's judgement). One variety of it comes from the Lower Carboniferous of the Meuse Valley; another from the uppermost Devonian of the same region. Both are deformed and altered by the stresses which formed the folds and thrust faults of the Ardennes; both are true marbles.

Bucklersbury House extends to the line of the Walbrook valley and the street of the same name, both

Tower of St Stephen Walbrook, showing the broken 'skin' of Portland Stone overlying the core of Ragstone and other materials.

falling to the level of the Thames close to Cannon Street Station. On the east bank of the stream course, stands the tower of **St. Stephen Walbrook (15)**, a mediaeval church of the City, modified by Wren after the Great Fire of 1666 in a very special way. In planning and superintending the work throughout himself, in itself an unusual thing, Wren is said to have worked out in this confined rectangular site the proportions of a domed structure, later to be scaled up for use in St Paul's. The interior too is exceptional for the richness of the mouldings and the ornamentation which would glorify any cathedral. However, it is the external walling which is of interest to us, and its composite nature. This can be seen in the flanks of the tower, but more extensively in the long wall to Bond Court. Here, the church can be seen to be built of irregular shaped blocks of Kentish Rag, with occasional pieces of flint, Roman brick, and what is possibly Caen Stone from Normandy (a pale-coloured, fine grained limestone, here cross-striated to take a plaster rendering). Probably very little of this surface would have been seen in the original church because of the pressing in of adjacent buildings, but the wall and tower visible from Walbrook were clearly later encased in good quality Portland Stone (a thin skin, breached at several points in the present condition of the church), with the same stone in solid masonry forming the elaborate pinnacles capping the steeple.

At the junction between Bucklersbury and Walbrook, stands a different kind of geological monument. **The Bank of New Zealand (16)** is another of the triangular-plan buildings which ingeniously adjust to the street plan of this quarter. It has some claim to merit architecturally in its massive and solid appearance, with heavy rustication and some rather fearsome bearded heads ornamenting the keystones to the window arches. In all this, the Bank could be said to be typical of its time (1873) when, as Summerson has said, banking and insurance were obliged to boast of their reliability and soundness through the rock-sound solidity of their exteriors. Sombre though it may be in colour, we can appreciate the Bank of New Zealand as that rare thing in the City, a building of sandstone, and a sandstone of uncommon nature from

Minera in the North Wales coalfield, close to Wrexham. Although brown overall, the sandstone has variable colour tone because of a kind of 'watermark' ringing to the blocks, an effect produced by the mobilisation of colouring iron oxides within the beds. The grain size is quite coarse—sufficient to merit the term 'grit' in some blocks. Yet another interest is the weathering characteristics of the stone, where weaknesses have provoked conspicuous dental repairs to corners and projections around the building.

If the Bank deserves a special geological preservation order against threatened redevelopment, as much, if not more, can be said for the offices and shops opposite which make up **Mansion House Buildings (17)**, better known as Mappin & Webbs' from the premises which occupy the prow of the wedge facing Mansion House and The Royal Exchange. The buildings were put up in 1870 to the design of Belcher and Belcher, and must represent everyone's idea of Victorian Gothic architecture, with each floor heavy with decorative ornament of one kind or another. The windows of each of the four floors differ in their tracery and surround details, but always involve shafts of stone as mullions and arch supports. Wherever possible it seems, stone has been carved into decorations in the shape of animals or grotesques—details easily executed in the freestone-quality Bath Stone which is the prevailing rock type of the entire building. In the shafting to the windows, it is supplemented by pale red New Red Sandstone (now overpainted, following the recent refurbishment of the whole block). Yet another touch of stone comes between the arches to the first floor, in the form of polished hemispheres of Peterhead Granite, bulging from the walls like carbuncles. A final gem is the principal entrance from Queen Victoria Street—a High Gothic portal, flanked by shafts of Peterhead Granite, supported by strange mythical beasts seemingly straight from the canvases of Hieronymous Bosch. These, the coats of arms, and the heads of Gog and Magog craning from the porthole-like roundels above the doorway, are all examples of the use of artificial stone pastes of the kind manufactured by Doultons of Lambeth to replicate what in other times would have been days of work

Mappin & Webb's, part of Mansion House Buildings; mainly Bath Stone, with window shafts of New Red Sandstone.

for a master mason working in natural stone.

Although these buildings together with The Bank of New Zealand, carry Grade II preservation orders as buildings of architectural merit, they have for several years been under threat by redevelopment of the whole area from Pancras Lane to Poultry to the north, and Bucklersbury to the south (the Palumbo Plan). The proposals which threaten them foresee their clearance and the creation of a wide pedestrian piazza. To one side would stand a tower unit after a surviving plan of Mies van der Rohe, which for its size and threat to the existing skyline of the area, has already caused serious disquiet in the City. The effect of completing the Palumbo Plan has been calculated by Arthur Kutchner in a series of sketch-projections (1976, 1978), and referred to by John Harris (1982) with gloomy prediction as to the inappropriateness of Italian-style piazza open spaces in our windswept London. Had we a geological vote on what might happen here, it must be clear that I would lead any campaign for diverse natural stone as seen in the existing buildings, and be against

Bank of England; the Herbert Baker south face in Portland Stone.

anything which would see the substitution of metal and glass, with only token facings of marble to foyers and lift shafts.

After such a whiff of controversy, **The Mansion House (18)** raises no comparable fire. It probably deserves more attention for its architecture and historical significance than for its geology, except to say that it clearly represents Portland Stone of mid-18th century date, weathered over two centuries, and still in good order in most parts of the fabric. Heavily rusticated at ground floor level, the building does involve several blocks of the Dorset stone, which must approach the maximum cube and linear dimensions available from the well-known quarry sections. Remember, the stone is quarried from horizontal bedded units of solid stone, separated by softer, flakey limestone or even clay bands, which have to be trimmed away from the usable heart-stone. Lateral limits to blocks are set by the vertical joints which subdivide the same beds. Both sets of limitations mean that there is less scope to cut Portland Stone to the unit sizes possible with some granites or sandstones, and more need to employ masons skills in matching and joining smaller blocks to form the massive pillars seen here.

As it is, Mansion House provides a platform from which we can review the appearance of the same Portland Stone in an almost continuous panorama around the Bank intersection. Our starting point could be the **Bank of England** itself, directly opposite. What we see is actually the South Screen, the surviving fragment of Soane's original Bank of the late 18th century, surmounted by the sheer mass of the much later Bank of Sir Herbert Baker (1921–37)—all very white. To the right is the classical columnate portico of **The Royal Exchange**, built in 1844 and, at present, slightly grimy in its Portland Stone. Some would argue, however, that the black-and-whiteness of the fluted columns lends a three-dimensional solidity which has effect. An answer to this might be to note the splendid appearance across Cornhill of **The Royal Insurance Office** designed by McVicar Anderson in 1905, which was recently cleaned. North west of Mansion House, stands the sheer white wall of **The National Westminster Bank,** originally The National Provincial Bank when built by Sir Edwin Cooper (**19**). This Bank is a strange mix of architectural details, right up to the crowning superstructure, but throughout it is a demonstration of good-quality Base- or Whit-Bed Portland Stone, with a limited amount of shell debris to break its freestone character after some fifty years of weathering. Equally white and massive in character is the Poultry Branch of **The Midland Bank** next door (**20**), designed by Lutyens with skilful proportions for the perspectives of the narrow street. Here again we find the freestone qualities of Portland Stone demonstrated in the carvings

National Westminster Bank, junction of Poultry with Princes St.

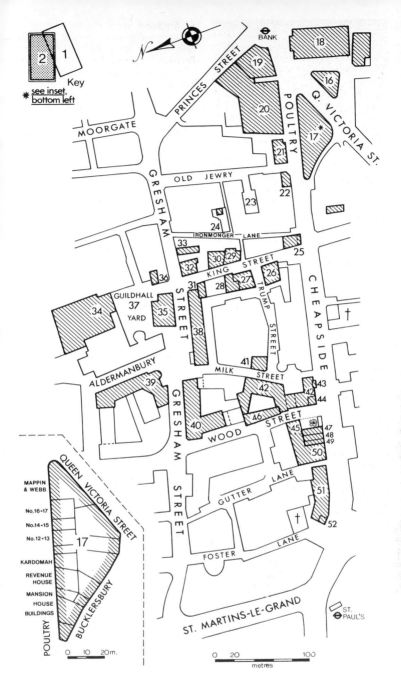

which embellish the keystones to the ground floor windows, as well as in the statues which complete the first floor terminations. Both Banks show the dazzling whiteness of this limestone as it weathers over the years, the original fresh-hewn stone being of a creamy-buff colour in the first instance, This same stone and the same whiteness continue into the next building in Poultry, **The Scottish Life Assurance** office (**21**). This is of much more recent date, as may be gathered from the flat-relief sculpture of Mitzi Cunliffe—appropriately Scottish Lions rampant and eagles.

At this point, we can rest our eyes from the dazzling whiteness of Portland Stone by looking from the north side of Poultry to the upper floors of Mansion House Buildings, continued through from Queen Victoria Street and adjoining Mappin & Webb's. Here we find some strange combinations of materials, predominantly of brown, red or yellow colour tones. As is common for redeveloped Victorian streets, we can see a strong unconformity between the new (and sometimes garish) at street level, and the solid core of the original building, which remains little disturbed above ground floor level. In these situations, it is instructive to stand back and look at such streets from the other pavement, if only to appreciate original uses and character. Looking to the south side of Poultry, next to Mappin's, we first see a narrow building in red brick with red sandstone and terracotta dressings, including tablets which tell us the street numbers as **Nos. 16–17**, and that the premises were once a Glovers shop. Next door, above **Dunhills**, the upper floors are of Bath Stone, with alternate round- and flat arches above the windows at successive floors. An improvised drain-pipe from the third floor has produced damage from penetrative dampness, not just to the Bath Stone, but also to the New Red Sandstone of the office next door (No. 13). Here, the detail to note is the exuberant use of terracotta in the broad horizontal panels across the frontage. The panels bear a relief frieze which represents the pageantry of the City of London through History. At first floor level, we have a youthful Queen Victoria in a mounted procession, succeeded at second floor by a Royalist scene. The third floor appears to represent Elizabethan times, while the fourth takes us back to Chaucer's Canterbury Pilgrims. Characteristically, all the details of this moulded sculpture remain crisp and clear in contrast to the crumbling sandstone course above the modern shop front. Moving up the street, the frontage above **The Kardomah Cafe** is pure Venetian, with balconied windows and cornices—all in Bath Stone once again. By contrast, Nos. 7–8 **Revenue House**, is very simple in style, with only slightly bowed windows running from floor to floor. The building material is rather grimy ceramic tile, with panels of dark serpentinite at the ground floor entrance, backing the shell-vault moulding. Finally, almost the last of these units which together form Mansion House Buildings as a whole, turns out to be the most restless in style and colour contrasts. At all floors, the walling is of pale yellow brick, but in the mouldings and window arches, this is set off by brickwork of contrasting colour, and fittings of artificial stone. In this last material there are roundels with heads in strong relief, there are shafts and moulded capitals—all drawn from the stock-in-trade of Doultons Lambeth Works. In themselves, perhaps only one or two of these premises would deserve a second thought when redevelopment is being discussed but, as we see in Cannon Street and Eastcheap in later walks, when they remain together as a survival of one period of time, they have infinitely greater merit. What could be conserved here would be a small sector of a Victorian street, with a diversity of buildings and building materials which would always be of interest to the geologist.

Moving up Poultry towards Cheapside, notice the serpentinite panels at street level fronting **The Trustee Savings Bank** at the junction with Old Jewry (**22**). From the colour contrasts, it is not difficult to recognise that the green 'cores' to the panels are original basic-to-ultrabasic material being made-over to the surrounding purple, heavily veined end-product of the processes of

Terracotta panels facing No. 13 Poultry; north side Mansion House Buildings.

The varied frontages to Mansion House Buildings, Poultry.

metamorphism. Serpentinite is a much-used facing stone for modern buildings, cut as thin sheets from quarried blocks. When you consider the rich colouring, and the fascinating veined patterns which we see here, the reason for its popularity are self-evident.

A detour up Old Jewry takes us away from Cheapside in order to gain two insights into a rather different London surviving from the past. A short distance up Old Jewry for example, we come to **Fredericks Place (23)**, a short cul-de-sac framed by town houses of the late 18th century. Not only are these a contrast in scale to the surrounding, towering commercial blocks, but also to the Victorian town houses which we see off Cannon Street (in the next walk). These are surviving designs of the Adam brothers (Pevsner dates them as 1776 in 'Buildings of England', 1962). Slipping round the corner from this quiet backwater, **St Olave's Court** connects Old Jewry with Ironmonger Lane, and takes us past a railed open space which was once the churchyard of St Olave's Jewry (**24**), a church demolished in 1888. What survives, however, in this tight-knit area, is a Wren tower of the church with a brick extension tacked on to it quite ingeniously. Viewed from Ironmonger Lane, it is at first a little disconcerting to see the curtained windows breaking the smooth face of the tower, but both this touch of the unexpected, and the quiet space the

re-use presents in the midst of a busy quarter of the City, make it worth while knowing about the 'Court'.

Ironmonger Lane leads us back to Cheapside, and a view of average quality buildings, of predictable geology. Alongside us on the north side is an exception in the form of **Atlas House (25)**, a very solid structure built for one of the earliest Insurance Companies by the architect Thomas Hopper in 1836. Like The Bank of New Zealand in Queen Victoria Street (Stop **16** above), Atlas House fulfils all that one would ask of a model of reliable, solid worth. This is achieved in massive blocks of Cornish Granite, rough-dressed to add still further to the impression of soundness—the soundness of a Cornish sea-wall against Atlantic waves. The building was gutted during the War, was rebuilt, and is now internally refitted yet again (1983), but what survives and will always catch the eye is the deep arcade of granite arches which extends across the pavement to Cheapside. Here you can see through the rough surface-finish, that the granite is in fact one of the large feldspar varieties from the south west, an example of which would be Lamorna Granite from the Lands' End district. The actual source of the stone for Atlas House is not known, but the upper floors are of Portland Stone yet again.

Atlas House stands at the foot of King Street, a relatively straight route cut in Wren's rebuilding of the City to connect Guildhall with Thameside. Geologically, its buildings are suficiently interesting to draw us northwards, commencing with **Nos. 36–37 King Street (26)**, a Victorian office of Baroque mass and style, involving several different types of natural stone. There is for example, Portland Stone at ground level, followed upwards by Bath Stone at first floor above. The colour contrasts of these sedimentary rocks is heightened by the stout columns of dark grey Rubislaw Granite, coupled with the browner-toned Kemnay Granite in pillars on either side of the entrance. Both granites are from that prolific source of British granites, Aberdeenshire.

Across Trump Street, the **Mitsui Bank** shows a Black Gabbro at pavement level, combined with pale coloured Portland Stone above (**27**)—a rather conventional combination these days. Much less common are the sheets of marble which face the premises of **The Bayerisches Landesbank** next door (**28**). This rock is the Carboniferous Limestone from the Pas de Calais of northern France, known as Napoleon Marble, and the variety called Tigre, on account of its striped pattern of lithologies. The marble is in fact a shallow-water algal limestone, with some of the banded character of travertines, but differing from that rock type in being fossiliferous (mainly marine gastropods), and including in its banding those dense carbonate layers which we recognise as being of algal origin. The tiger-striping which gives the name Tigre, has all the evidence of being the result of shrinkage-cracking produced by drying out of the lime-mud shortly after deposition, the cracks later becoming infilled by clear white calcite. Such a shallow-water environment would be quite in keeping with the presence of calcareous algae.

Switching to the other side of King Street, we have the opportunity to compare a large-feldspar Cornish Granite of the Lamorna type in two contrasting finishes. In **The Leicester Building Society** (**29**), the door surround is of polished granite, with the large orthoclase feldspar crystals clearly visible. In **The Banco do Brasil** next door (**30**), the same feldspars are less easy to pick out in the fine-axe dressed finish to the same stone. **No. 16 King Street**, again the premises of Banco do

Banca Commerciale Italiana, King Street; Portland Stone.

Brasil, offers a spectacular exposure of a lightly figured White Marble in the deep-set arches which front the building. Pale grey colour banding within the marble picks out swirling patterns across the surfaces as evidence of the deformation which the rock has undergone. Its source is unknown, although it is possible that it may even be from Brazil, as both granite and marble are now an important part of the export trade from that country. A national Bank could well be a shop window to demonstrate just this fact. What is undisputed is the impact which this marble frontage has in the building pattern of King Street, especially on a sunny afternoon.

More conventional marble is part of the fitting to **The Bank of Detroit** (**31**), which otherwise has some very elegant columns of pink Peterhead Granite enhancing its frontage. Looking at this Bank at closer quarters, however, is a pretext for setting up a view of a remarkable survival of Victorian commercial architecture on the opposite pavement—No. 42 Gresham Street, **The Banca Nazionale d'Italia** (**32**). Geologically, it is all very straightforward, being entirely of Portland Stone, but its treatment by the architect Sancton Wood involved heavy rustication and vermiculation of the stonework, and a wealth of decorative carving to give it a throughly Italian Renaissance look. It was in fact built for The Queen's Insurance Company in 1858, hence the image of the young Victoria above the first floor window on the angle facing Guildhall. Sympathetically cleaned, and enriched by the carved wooden doors, it is a splendid building.

Equally noteworthy, and of the same general age, is **The Iranian Bank Saderat** next door in Gresham Street (**33**), which is very similar to the Italian Bank in its upper floors. What is of interest to us is the reconstruction of the ground floor entrance which has introduced a strongly figured red marble into the deep-arched windows and doorway. The deep cherry-red colour of the stone, offset by the contrasting white calcite veining, is the source of the name Griotte Vive Flamme ('griotte' = cherry in Italian) for this Belgian marble. The 'Griotte' marbles are worked from quarries within the reef limestone masses of the Upper Devonian of the Meuse Valley. The depth of the colour varies according to the height above the reef base (deeper red at the base, becoming paler upwards in the structure). A close look at the polished surfaces here will not reveal very much in the way of identifiable fossil material other than crinoid ossicles, but what do stand out clearly are grey triangular patches, perhaps lines by calcite crusts, which are recognisable as *Stromatactis*. Of a possible combined algal/foraminiferal origin these *Stromatactis* structures have become diagnostic of reef carbonates in the Palaeozoic. Otherwise, the marble is criss-crossed by creamy white calcite masses which reflect the recrystallisation of the original limestone rock, and the deformation which the Devonian succession of the Ardennes suffered during the Hercynian Orogeny.

The Guildhall; Kentish Rag walling, Collyweston Slate roofing.

Returning to the junction between King Street and Gresham Street, we see facing us to the north, **The Guildhall**, a focal point for the City and its rebuilding following savage War damage. In its present form this area has become a broad paved space, flanked by the Corporation Church of St Lawrence Jewry, the new Guildhall Library and Museum, the Guildhall itself and a series of surviving Victorian offices.

Oldest of these, The Guildhall (**34**) with its complicated building history, has the simplest geology. It is essentially of Kentish Rag, dressed in slightly bulging and flaking blocks. This is not too easy to see at close quarters on account of the glass-fronted cloister to the Museum, and the canopied entrance to the main hall, but a short detour into Basinghall Street sees the slightly gritty and glauconite-speckled limestone down at pavement level in the supporting buttresses for convenient study. Glauconite is a mineral with a distinctive dark green colour. Its presence in Kentish Rag tells us that this was a marine sediment, laid down in shallow-water, near-shore conditions before the deposition of the Chalk in southern England. The Victorian gothicising of the mediaeval Guildhall, saw the introduction of Portland Stone into the portico with its pinnacles and coats of arms, as well as into the upright buttresses strengthening the whole structure. It is worthwhile looking up to the steep-pitched roof of the hall to note the grey-green slates, visibly thicker and more lumpy than normal roof slating. They are in fact Collyweston Slates, frost-split tiles of fissile Lincolnshire Limestone from the Welland Valley west of Stamford. Unlike true slates, these are unaltered sedimentary rocks, tough and impermeable enough to make suitable though weighty roofing material.

Kentish Rag is also to be seen in the walling to **St Lawrence Jewry** (**35**) which faces on to the Guildhall piazza. Rough blocks of rag, Flint, Roman brick and unidentifiable rubble have been left exposed in the rebuilding of the bomb-shattered church (restored between 1954–57). In the west tower and the walling to Gresham Street, we see the same Wren skin of white Portland Stone which we have already seen in St Stephen Walbrook (stop **15**) covering the functional walling with a more attractive external facing. Of this exterior, it is particularly interesting to look at the blocks at the base of the west tower to see that they still bear the metal comb dressing of the original mason-work, so evidencing minimal loss of surface over two centuries of weathering. Nearby we can equally clearly see the black and white contrasts and loss of surface which different aspect and exposure to wind and rain can produce in the same stone.

Turning now to the Victorian offices facing the east end of the church, those of the Estate Agent, **Baker, Harries & Sanders** (**36**) have recently been cleaned and show Portland Stone at ground floor level

Diamant Granulite paving to Guildhall courtyard.

passing up into Bath Stone in the upper floor—both stones appropriate and conventional for the time of building. As much could not be said of the paving of the open space which now fronts The Guildhall for while tradition might have seen conventional sized squares of York Stone, here we have smaller tablets of a micaceous rock of several different colours—grey, buff, and pinkish-red (**37**). The rock is Diamant Schist, or perhaps more correctly, Diamant Granulite, imported from Namaqualand on the margins of the Kalahari Desert of South West Africa. Although it may look scaly and irregular in surface, the rock is extremely tough and hard-wearing, being an original sediment which has undergone intense metamorphism at a later date, heat and pressure having fused and welded the sand grains into this indurated quartz-rock. Lines of blue-black dolerite setts separating the expanses of Diamant flags, further diversify the pattern of this courtyard area, geologically so unique.

Leaving the Guildhall, and returning to Gresham Street, **Nos. 20–40** make up one of several blocks grouped hereabout which take us back to the building modes of the Fifties (**38**). In this particular building, it is the bands of strongly coloured tile-mosaic which catch the eye in the upper floors. At pavement level, there are inserts of white quartzite in small, flat pieces, broken across with conchoidal fracture, and set up with a brick-work pattern like a fireplace surround. More interesting, and very much a sign of the time of building are the columns and wall panels lining the main entrance which show off beautifully the character of Derbyshire Fossil Marble. This is not a true 'marble', but rather a brown limestone, crowded with the cylindrical sections of crinoid ossicles, which, when cut across, give the 'figure' to the polished surfaces. The stone (sometimes called Dene Stone), comes from quarries between Wirksworth and Cromford in Derbyshire and gained universal approval in Britain after its prominent use for the interior walling of The Royal Festival Hall, built on the South Bank for the 1951 Festival of Britain. For a time, after 1951, it became a popular choice to add a touch of richness to otherwise simple, stone-clad buildings otherwise short on colour. As with other stones after a time, it lost some of its novelty and at the same time became less easy to acquire from the original quarry. In this way, it now assumes a kind of hallmark for the years 1951 to 1956, a kind of building stone fossil identifying a unit of geological time.

Across the intersection of Gresham Street and Aldermanbury, the second of the these buildings of the Fifties is **Barrington House** (**39**), a banking and office development of 1954–56. At pavement level, there

Barrington House, Aldermanbury; granite base panels, fluted pillars of Torquay Marble, upper walls of Portland Stone.

are massive, roughly-finished blocks of dark grey granite of unknown source. No such problem of provenance attaches to the dark and veined marble which forms the free-standing columns to the first floor base. These are of Torquay Marble from South Devon. The rock is a Middle Devonian limestone, altered by regional deformation, as was the Belgian 'Griotte' seen earlier (stop **33**), but not to such a degree as to destroy all trace of a rich fauna of corals and calcareous algae. These now stand out paler against the velvet-black background of the muddy limestone. To add a quality which makes this rock the nearest approach to the classic antique marbles of Greece and Rome there are deep red veins penetrating the Torquay stone. The remaining upper surfaces of Barrington House are clad in Portland Stone, but of two distinct varieties. The greater areas of the vertical surface are clad with the normal Whit- or Base-Bed limestone, of even-grain smoothness, but crossing these surfaces as narrow bands, are strips of Portland Roach— the limestone crowded with casts of fossil gastropods and bivalves to give a very contrasted rough texture.

Detail of veined Torquay Marble.

Opposite Barrington House, at the junction of Milk Street with Gresham Street, **Clement's House** (now Byblos Bank SAL), built also in the years 1954–56, is the third of the local offices of the same time period, and it is in some senses the most spectacular in its stonework (**40**). Like the others, it is a steel-framed building to which natural stone is attached as cladding in relatively thin slabs. Much of the stone facing is of Portland Stone, but more prominent are vertical strips which are cleavage

Front wall to Clement's House, Gresham Street; vertical strips and mosaic panels of Barge Quartzite.

splits of Italian Barge Quartzite. These are attached to the frame by conspicuous bolts and washers, visible at each contact of the relatively small slabs. This so-called quartzite is really another granulite (as was the case with Diamant Schist earlier) from the Italian Alpes Maritimes (Monte Bracco), the colour varying slightly according to the split of the cleavage. Some surfaces are covered with muscovite mica and so are silvery-grey; others are faced with smears of white or rusty coloured quartz, and can be either grey

Detail of Barge Quartzite, Clement's House.

47

or yellowish accordingly. Otherwise, the standard colour for the rock is buff. Irregular shapes and off-cuts of the same stone make up the unusual (and hideous) mosaic panels which run across the floor levels like artificial snake-skin belts. One other detail which could easily be overlooked is the limestone which lines the deep-set windows at ground floor level. This is a limestone of marble-quality which is crowded with the dark brown shells of rudistid bivalves. As with other examples of this faunal association seen in London buildings, this is another rock which is 'exotic' to Britain, probably coming from Mediterranean sources.

Milk Street leads us back towards Cheapside, passing on the left hand side the refitted **State Bank of India** (**41**), resplendent in a highly polished stopped travertine which glows like strongly grained wood. Inside, the Bank is floored with the cream coloured Italian Perlato Marble, crowded with small fossil bryozoa and corals, as well as the more obvious brown shell fragments of bivalves.

Opposite the Bank, on the right side of Milk Street, the extensive premises of **Schröder-Wagg** (**42**) are interesting for the panels of coarsely crystalline granite which split the floor levels. The rock has a porphyritic texture in which large buff feldspars are picked out and emphasised by the concentration of black grains of ferromagnesian minerals. Both the colour contrasts and the mineral texture of this rock are distinctive, and seem to point to

it being an Italian granite known as Serizzo Ghiandone of Oligocene age from Sondrio in the Italian Alps. The location in the Rhaetian Alps, up-valley from Lake Como, and the age, all help to explain the altered state of the large feldspars and the measure of crushing which is evident in these polished surfaces.

The paved walk from Milk Street brings us back to Cheapside alongside a Jewellers shop (**43**), which is something of a jewel in itself for the rich coloured Walnut Rubane Travertine which faces it. Not only is this Spanish travertine a richer colour than that seen in The State Bank of India, but the structures are more varied. In places, the layers are buckled and folded; in places the buckling may extend to actual rupture with the formation of bands of limestone breccia. Altogether, the patterns here are fascinating, and could be studied for hours.

The **Panam Office** next door, No. 122 Cheapside (**44**), brings back the large-feldspar granite, this being an extension of the Schröder-Wagg building from Milk Street (**42**). At this point, we are drawn northwards once again to look at **Three Keys House** (**45** just beyond the open space which used to be the churchyard of St Peter Cheap, a pre-Fire church, cleared and never rebuilt after 1666. Three Keys House was completed in 1982 by the architects T. P. Bennett, effectively combining the distinctive Italian Sardinian Beige Granite in polished panels with the rough-textured Portland Roach in the champfered verticals of the upper

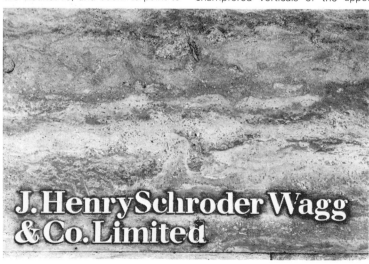

Detail of Walnut Rubane Travertine, entrance to Schröder-Wagg's.

floors. The foyer to the building is lined and fitted out with another variety of travertine, confusingly called Florentine Travertine, but said to come from Sicily.

Compter House on the other side of Wood Street (**46**), an office block of the Fifties, offers horizontal cladding strips between the floors of Lake District Green Slate. This rock is strictly a fine-grained volcanic ash which has been cleaved and altered in the course of the folding experienced by the Lake District succession. Blocks are quarried utilising the vertical joint planes which cross the beds, and are then sawn usually with the cleavage direction so that true bedding emerges as colour banding running across the slabs. Some of the panels of Compter House show not only this bedding, but also its disturbance as a result of contemporaneous slumping or the rupture anf faulting of the wet ash. Several of these slate panels are interesting in this way, and are seen here to good effect when afternoon sun plays upon the surfaces.

Back in Cheapside once more, **Williams & Glyn's Bank** at No. 127, (**47**) has good surfaces of a fine-grained, grey-blue granodiorite which may be one of the Dalbeattie-Kircudbright intrusions of the Southern Uplands of Scotland—a suite of rocks which tend to have this finer grain size to their minerals, as well as the grey-blue tone on account of their lower proportion of free quartz. Possibly greater interest attaches to the granite facings of the premises next door (**48**). Here we have red granite pillars on bases of almost black granite, but the red granites do not match across the frontage. The red granite of **No. 129** (**49**) for example is the familiar pink granite from Peterhead, while that of No. 128 is the deeper toned red Virgo Granite from Vanevik in Sweden, clearly recognisable for its blue quartz crystals. The near-black granite of the bases is Cairngall Granite, a variety of the Peterhead intrusion. Its relationship to the more normal pink rock is given away by the presence of pink orthoclase feldspar crystals in the otherwise dark rock. These are geologically interesting points in buildings which by any standards would be regarded as ordinary, and one can't help feeling that this stopping point of our itinerary might be swept away by redevelopment at any time.

The combination of Sardinian Beige Granite with Portland Roach, seen earlier in Three Keys House, returns in Cheapside in the extension of that new building into the premises of **John Collier** and **Richard Shops** (**50**). Normal Portland Stone cladding also returns in **Cheapside House** (**51**), the headquarters of Lonrho, but is enriched in the entrance foyer by walling of gold-toned Italian Stopped Travertine from Tivoli Quarries outside Rome. Beyond Lonrho, a detail of interest arises in the facings to **W. H. Smith & Sons** (**52**) where, in the gable end to Foster Lane, and in the uprights to Cheapside, we see a rusty-green weathering rock contrasting strongly with the white Portland slabs. This is flame-textured Larvikite, a rock which we are accustomed to seeing in its polished surface finish when its large feldspars flash with reflected light. This normal treatment is seen in narrow strips at pavement level which only serves to make the other treatment seem dismal. At this point, we have arrived at a link up with the ground covered in Walk 1. Looking around at the precinct to St Paul's, we can take in a wide range of building history, and an equally wide range of favoured building stones.

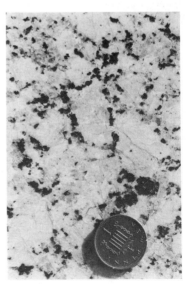

Serizzo Ghiandone Granite

Cannon Street from the Dome of St Paul's.

CANNON STREET

This walk commences roughly where the second walk ended, at the top of Queen Victoria Street, takes in almost the entire length of Cannon Street before turning back via Fenchurch Street and Lombard Street to The Royal Exchange and Bank, the starting point for the next walk.

Standing in front of Bracken House, the headquarters of 'The Financial Times', we are surrounded by buildings and planning decisions which speak of the 1950's. First, there is the open space of Festival Gardens to the east of St Paul's, set out to celebrate the Festival of Britain in 1951 at the same time as traffic was re-routed along the curving line of New Change. The distinctive form of the transplanted Choir School was the bright invention of a later decade (1963), otherwise most of the other buildings in sight bear the distinctive marks of a 'period' as recognisable as the fashion in clothing of the time. Watling House, The Bank of England New Change, Gateway House, No. 20 Cannon Street, and Scandinavian House all have in common rather square outlines, set four-square to the road plan in a kind of post-Austerity economy of space which was lost in the Sixties. What they also share is a limited range of stone types, often used with a startling contrast of colour or texture, a practice which happily died out quite quickly in the years which followed. Invariably, the basic rock used would be Portland Stone in a smooth ashlar finish against which would be set rough-surfaced Lake District slate, buff-coloured York Stone or brightly coloured ceramic tile. Many of these touches can be seen in the buildings mentioned, all of which sprang up in the systematic redevelopment of the area following war-time damage. As we proceed along Cannon Street, we will recognise the types again, but there interspersed with surviving Victorian elements of quite a different colour palette, and later date additions which have been much more adventurous in both design and their use of exotic rock types.

In looking at buildings in more detail, we can start with **Gateway House**, New Change (**1**) now the premises of Bank of America but originally the offices of Wiggins Teape. With change of ownership some of the original stonework and fittings have been changed from what was seen in 1956 when the building was new. The main walling is still of contrasting brown and orange brick, now set off at ground level by panels of cream-coloured stopped travertine which extends into the pillars which support the through-passage and floor the entrance to the Bank. Low down in the wall, rough-riven slabs of grey-blue slate (probably Burlington Slate from the southern Lake District) present both a colour and textural contrast to the smooth surfaces of travertine—a typical Fifties touch.

In passing, a further word about **Bracken House** (**2**), already commented upon at the close of the second walk. It too is a building of the Fifties, designed by Sir Albert Richardson in 1958, but it in no way does it follow the pattern of Gateway House, being built of a good quality russet-brown brick, combined with a rich red sandstone. This sandstone is Hollington Stone from the Triassic outcrops of north Staffordshire and is the stone which was chosen for the restoration of Coventry Cathedral at the end of the War. The current-bedding and the weathering of the stone over the years have already been commented upon, but as we now look at the northern face of the building it is timely to mention details of the interior of the 'Financial Times' building. The foyer is enriched by a variety of decorative marbles, a black crinoidal limestone from the Carboniferous forming a chequerboard pattern with a paler buff toned limestone of the same age, Hopton Wood Stone. Table tops in the entrance area, are surfaced with slabs of the striking Portoro Marble from the Siena district of Apennine Italy, an intensely black limestone criss-crossed with veins of amber coloured calcite. The total effect is quite rich, and reminiscent of an Edwardian Bank eager to press its opulence upon the potential client (**3**). About two years ago (1981) when the present walk was in a reconnaissance stage, **No. 20** (**3**) was yet another utility building of what we have come to recognise as a 1950's style although it was actually built in 1960. Clad with Portland Stone, there were in addition, attached panels of concrete, faced with angular fragments of grey-green dolerite, and for further colour and textural contrast, there were at ground floor level walling infills of York Stone slabs. After a life of twenty years all of this has passed away in a total renewal and now the building is a simpler, cleanlined addition to the local townscape. As it now is, there are strong horizontals of alloy sheeting and tinted glass, but at ground level there is a near-continuous sheet wall of polished 'Black Granite' known as Assoluta Black, which I am told is another name for Belfast Black, both being further examples of a South African Bushveld Gabbro. The fact that the rock can carry an obviously Italian name simply reflects the current situation in the stone trade, whereby quarry-cut blocks from all parts of the World are shipped to Italy where a great proportion of the cutting, polishing and finishing of facing stone takes place. The resulting names can be elegant and sometimes informative on the appearance of a stone, but sadly it adds just one further pitfall as we try to identify rock in buildings with a geographical source area. Like all 'Black Granites' the stone of No. 20 in bright sunlight, allows us to note the absence of the mineral quartz (hence the original rock was not a true granite), and also the fact that the feldspar minerals are heavily peppered with inclusions of opaque minerals to the extent that the rock has assumed its black colour. The shape of the feld-

spars is outlined by metallic screens of ore minerals, including the chromite which is worked commercially in the Bushveld outcrop. In fact, 'Black Granite' of very much the same character could be found in most of the older Precambrian Shield areas which make up the cores of the continents and our rock could have come from the Brazilian Shield close to Rio, from the Atlas Mountains of Morocco, from the Baltic Shield of Finland or the Deccan of South India—in this case, the record says 'South Africa'.

In its new form, No. 20 Cannon Street has several affinities with the building which stands alongside it, the premises of **Credit Lyonnais**. Both are buildings of black and white contrasts, both are bold and of clean lines; both are by the same architect.

Moving on to No. 30 Cannon Street, the headquarters of Credit Lyonnais (**4**), the striking black panels which cover much of the sheer exterior of this modern building (completed 1980), are another 'Black Granite' but this time specifically an African rock, Nubian Black, a very fine-grained Gabbro-type rock from the Bushveld region of the Transvaal. Viewed in slightly oblique light, lath-shaped crystals which were originally feldspars are picked out by delicate screens of ore minerals as part of the replacement process mentioned above. Combined with the silver alloy surfaces of the window surrounds, this black gleaming stone creates an imposing character for this building, placed as it is at one of the most strategically

Watling House, Cannon Street (Midland Bank centre right).

important positions in the City, framing views of St Paul's from the east. The interiors of the Bank are lightened by the extensive use of golden-toned travertine for the steps, counters and wall panels to the Banking Hall.

Watling House on the north side of Cannon Street opposite (**5**), reverts to the pattern typical for the Fifties, combining Portland Stone with green Lake District Slate, but adding a garish touch through strong horizontal strips of green ceramic times. The odd raised-domino detail to the surfaces of the Portland Stone panels gives the impression that the whole building is a kind of Lego-fantasy.

towards Cannon Street show a scaly exfoliation weathering, demonstrating the fact that even this normally sound stone can suffer deep disruption under conditions of penetrative damp. The result is a blister swelling of the surface, followed by an unsightly flaking of loosened slivers of stone. More has been said about St Mary's in the Cheapside walk.

The church stands at one of the focal points of City streets, created in 1871 when Queen Victoria Street was opened up from Blackfriars as a main traffic route to the heart of the City at The Royal Exchange. Carving a broad swathe through a pre-existing patterns which still survive truncated by its course, Queen Vic-

St Paul's from Cannon Street (Albert Buildings right).

At the foot of Bow Lane, extensive redevelopment of the Watling Court site occurred between 1980 and 1983, replacing a jumbled mix of small shops, cafes and Victorian offices with a large coordinated block grouped around **The Midland Bank**, all faced in a deep orange stopped travertine. Inevitably it impinges upon the Wren church of **St Mary Aldermary** (**6**) which has always been crowded out by other buildings, except for its tall tower with its Gothic pinnacles. The church was extensively damaged in the Great Fire, except for the base to the tower, and was subsequently rebuilt by Wren with the customary skin of smooth ashlar-finished Portland Stone encasing a rubble walling of predominantly Kentish Rag, flint and Roman brick. Some of the blocks of Portland Stone in the south wall

toria Street here intersects the line of Cannon Street, itself the result of road improvement work of 1846. At that time the City Architect J. B. Bunning sought to ease traffic westwards from Eastcheap and The Tower by a wide road crossing the Wallbrook stream and extending to Ludgate Hill. Contemporaneous with the 1870's road plan is the office block of **Albert Buildings** (**7**), built by F. J. Ward on an extended triangular site bounded by Queen Street, Cannon Street and the newly-opened Queen Victoria Street. This highly decorated piece of Victorian High Gothic architecture, rich in arcade windows as a Venetian palazzo, has a splendid dominance of the junction in all directions, now that it has been cleaned and refurbished. Most of its geological details are hidden beneath paintwork, but one

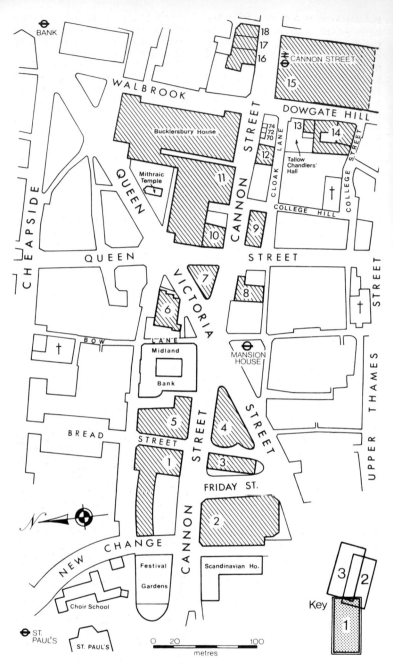

suspects that they include red sandstone shafts, polychrome brickwork and possibly stone dressings to the windows. In a strange way, the recently completed Credit Lyonnais buildings (**4** above), diametrically opposite and occupying a similarly difficult wedge-shaped space, seems to act as a counterbalancing unit to this classical Victorian office block.

Proceeding down Cannon Street, slightly set back from the line of the street, **The Royal Trust Company of Canada**, Nos 48–50, introduces the very distinctive Scandinavian rock, Baltic Brown Granite (**8**). The striking feature of this rock in polished surface is the occurrence of large crystals of pinkish-brown feldspar set against a darker brown groundmass of the rock as a whole.

Baltic Brown is a granite from Finland, where such rocks with this golf-ball texture are known as 'Rapakivi granites' forming a broad belt of outcrop across the Precambrian of southern Finland from the Gulf of Finland across to the Aland Islands in the Gulf of Bothnia. As a texture, we have something which can only be fully appreciated through having large surfaces to study as here in Cannon Street. In this modern building of 1977 not only the exterior is of geological interest, as the entrance foyer wall panelling and floor surface is of a pale limestone crowded with thick-shelled fossils which give it a marble figuring. The shells are of oyster-like bivalves known as rudists, which flourished in reef masses in the warm, limey seas of Cretaceous times. While the age is reasonably clear, the source of the particular limestone is less certain, but was probably Spain or a Mediterranean country from the known distribution of rudistid limestones.

Reaching Queen Street, we have come to one of the roads planned by Wren to give access to the City from Thames-side when he attempted his own solution to the problem of the rambling lanes and narrow streets of pre-Fire London. Its line continued in King Street beyond Cheapside, Queen Street leads directly to The Guildhall as one of the focal points of London. Today, Queen Street at this point is noteworthy for the restored-Georgian frontages of town houses, not forgetting the equally welcome trees which front them.

No. 52 Cannon Street opposite, **The American Express International-al Bank (9)**, forms the western end of a modern block which extends as far as College Hill, replacing Victorian shops and offices of 1846. In the new building Portland Stone at and above first floor levels is married with panels of 'Black Granite' at street level and about the entrance. Comparable with the stone of Credit Lyonnais (**4**) there is no certainty as to the provenance of this particular altered rock. Once again it appears to have been a coarsely crystalline igneous rock of Gabbro type, its minerals peppered with grains of metallic ores to the extent that they are now opaque and metallic themselves. Associated with, and in marked contrast to the black slabs, the bank interior is faced with the limpid white translucent marble, White Crystal. Metamorphism of the original limestone has here produced enlarged reformed crystals of calcite with no impurities to impart a body colour to the rock.

This building of the early 1970's contrasts strongly with that of **The London Chamber of Commerce and Industry** on the north side of Cannon Street opposite (**10**). Built in 1938 by Gunton & Gunton, this predates the mere cladding of steel framed buildings with a thin skin of natural stone and offers solid blocks of polished natural stone, recently cleaned and renovated. Like many commercial buildings, the lower courses and the entire ground floor are of solid granite, before passing up into walling of Portland Stone. The granite is the distinctive Lamorna Granite from Lands End, Cornwall, recognisable both for its colour and mineral texture. Its colour is grey-brown; its texture, strongly porphyritic, with large, elongate crystals of orthoclase feldspar set within a darker-hued groundmass. Other than the feldspars, minerals which can be recognised include dark-grey shapeless patches of quartz, and wisps of brownish-black biotite mica.

London Chamber of Commerce, Cannon Street

Alongside and overshadowing the London Chamber of Commerce, is the south wing of the large complex which is **Bucklersbury House (11)**, built between 1953 and 1958 by

Campbell-Jones and Partners. The long span of years of this development included a complicated clearance of the Victorian buildings which lined these City streets, and the re-siting of the Roman Mithraic Temple which was discovered in the course of foundation work on the banks of the Walbrook (see the Cheapside walk). Here on Cannon Street, Bucklersbury House provides large surface areas of polished Larvikite of a colour which is typical for stone worked from the quarries of the Larvik area in recent years. This stone is an electric blue rather than the more sombre, almost-jet black tone of older material, whilst the large feldspars show in strong relief the myriad of small inclusions which are in part responsible for the refraction of light and the production of the well-known shimmering iridescence of the large crystals. The upper walling is of Portland Stone of the even-textured Whit- or Base-Bed quality, the whole surfaces here suffering from the streaky downwash of lime and grime which drains down over the sheer surface.

Opposite Bucklersbury House is the Conservation Area of College Hill, connecting Cannon Street with Lower Thames Street and in a sense taking one back in time almost a century. In College Hill and Cloak Lane we can find what have been called,'the best small streets in the City, retaining something of a pre-Victorian atmosphere' (Fawcett, 1976), owing much to the separation away from the busy traffic of the main thoroughfare and the one-way system of access. The character of College Hill is very much a matter of good quality brickwork, well-proportioned windows and elegant door cases rather than stonework, but this only serves to set the comparison for the Victorian patterns of building which were to follow and which we would vote equally deserving of conservation, if only for their geological potential.

Returning to Cannon Street, there follows a section with several points of geological interest involving a combination of original Victorian brickwork and stone dressings, along with some ingenious modern refitting of shops and offices at ground floor levels. For example, in the premises of **Banco Totta & Acores**, and of **Mecca (12)**, there are broad surfaces of Swedish Carnation Red Granite in the door- and window-surrounds. Coming from the Precambrian Shield of southern Sweden, this rock is strongly foliated and its minerals show a distinct layering across the polished surfaces, broken by knot-like lenses at regular intervals. Closer examination of these same lenses will show them to be large crystals of feldspar, broken across by fracture planes as close set as in a sliced loaf. These shears and the streaked out layering tell that the original granitic rock was in its later history subjected to crushing stresses which transformed it into something of the nature of a gneiss—a metamorphic rock type. Having said that, it remains that the rock which we are looking at must lie mid-way between granite and gneiss, stressing the problems of rock classification.

The process of learning continues in the frontages of the next sequence of buildings, **Nos 70–74, Cannon Street**. Here we find a rock which is both fine-textured and dense in appearance, with a strong, almost unnatural purple colour. At first glance, it could be taken as being one of many modern synthetic stones made up from carefully chosen aggregates and pigmented to give it a distinctive appearance. This is a technique which commenced with the bonding of limestone chips in mortar to produce what we know as terrazo, and which now extends to a wider variety of mixes involving harder minerals such as quartz or flint. Quartz is certainly present here in angular to sub-angular grains, but elsewhere in this particular rock there are patches of coarser material which are more significant in assessing whether it is natural or artificial. The margins of these 'inclusions' show traces of marginal fusion which tend to suggest that this was a volcanic ash or tuff in which falling fragments became 'welded' together while the material was still hot. Whether this is a correct interpretation of what is before us as a quite elegant stone, is open to debate; neither a trade name nor a provenance are known to us, but it does serve to illustrate the problems posed by stone in buildings and a possible approach of reasoning from observed facts.

At this point, we have reached the line of the Walbrook, a narrow valley which is traceable through the built-up area of The City as a well-defined break in the contour of the streets,

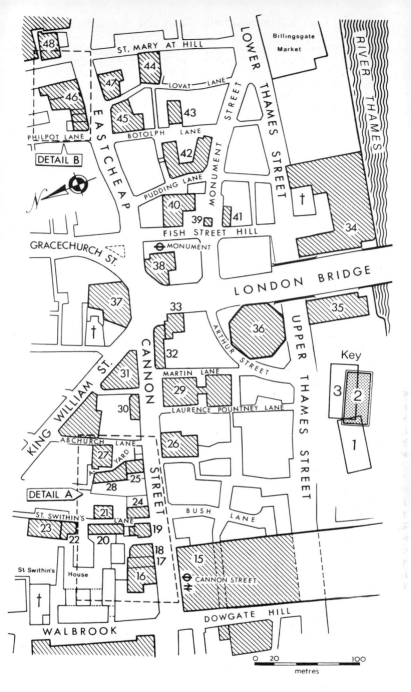

including such main thoroughfares as Cannon Street which visibly 'dip'. To the north, the valley is lined by tall buildings—Walbrook House to the east; Bucklersbury House to the west, both in Portland Stone. To the south, the line of the brook is continued as Dowgate Hill, flanked by the imposing surviving wall of the original Cannon Street Station (built in 1856), which, with its terminal tower overlooking the Thames, is one of the celebrated 'townscape' views in the City. Dowgate Hill also contains some interesting geological features which begin with the office block, **Drake House** just beyond Cloak Lane (**13**). Built of brick, with terracotta mouldings at ground floor level, the entrance and window surrounds are of Shap Granite. This reddish-brown rock is yet another example of a rock with porphyritic texture, the phenocrysts being large pink crystals of orthoclase feldspar set within a groundmass of smaller orthoclase crystals, some quartz, and small dark grains of hornblende. On these surfaces, a clear alignment of the feldspars suggests fluid-flow while the rock was still molten.

At street level, close to the second entrance to the same building (No. 6, Dowgate Hill), hinged panels giving access to the basement are worth a moments study as a piece of deception. The surface bears details of veining, and the clear outline of what look like fossil corals which would be appropriate for the Devonian Torquay Marble of south west England. Scanning the total area, however, it quickly registers that there is a repetition of some of the eye-catching detail as there would be in wall-paper designs, giving away the fact that these panels are a Formica-simulation of real stone.

Further down Dowgate Hill, beyond Drake House, are three of the Livery Halls of City Companies, all pre-dating the 19th Century and adding a touch of elegance to the local scene. **The Tallow Chandler's Hall** is largely hidden by Drake

Granite House & Barclays Bank

House, but shares a Shap Granite entrance porch, closed by gates of ornamental ironwork. **The Skinner's** (No. 8–9) and **The Dyer's Halls** (No. 10) follow in quick succession (**14**). Like many 18th Century buildings in the City, these are mainly brick buildings enhanced by plaster renderings and painted-overall.

The pilastered and pedimented frontage of The Skinner's Hall is a good example of the style. Geologically, there is little to draw attention to, but it is recorded in Pevsner that the sculptural detail of the pediment are of Coade Stone (Pevsner, 1962).

Returning to Cannon Street, we have now reached the **Railway Station (15)** which was redesigned from its 1865 simplicity by the architect Charles Poulson to its present form in 1961. The restructuring of the frontage to Cannon Street saw the introduction of large surface areas of Portland Roach—the richly shelly facies of the well-known building stone. In Roach, the actual shells have been largely dissolved away, leaving casts and internal cavities as sole evidence of their original presence. As a result the rock is porous and rough textured, but attractive to the would-be palaeontologist, seeking examples of the 'Portland Screw' (a high spired marine gastropod) or the hoof-like outline of the bivalve *Trigonia*.

Facing the station is **Granite House**, designed in 1975 by Whinney and Partners for Allied Arab Banks (**16**), which appropriately offers two 'granites' of contrasting types in its extensive surfaces of polished stonework. At pavement level, there are plinths of stone which resemble in some respects the 'Black Granites' of earlier buildings. This particular rock has a greyer tone overall, stemming from evenly distributed patches of quite un-altered feldspar laths grouped in clusters. Geologically, the rock is a gabbro, similar in mode of origin and to some extent texture to granite, but differing fundamentally in its chemical composition which is poor in silica. This expresses itself quite simply in the total absence of quartz as a recognisable mineral on any of these surfaces. The rock comes from the Bushveld Complex of the Transvaal, and is Rustenberg Bon Accord Gabbro. The second igneous rock of this Bank is the buff-brown stone known as Roxo Granite. As with all igneous rocks, it is the colour

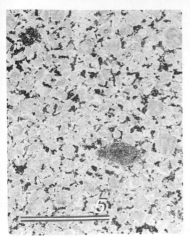

Detail of Roxo Granite, Granite House, Cannon Street. Scale in cm.

of the feldspar component which is responsible for the overall colour of the rock; here there are two types of feldspar (pinkish in colour) interlocking with a dark-green-to-black ferromagnesian mineral producing an intergrowth texture. As with the preceding Gabbro, again there is an absence of free quartz, which suggests that this rock too is not a true granite. Scanning the polished surfaces of this beautiful rock, there occur from time to time small dark inclusions of other material. These are xenoliths, incorporated fragments of the crustal rocks into which the granite was melting its way, fragments which were not completely assimilated before the final phase of cooling of the melt. Looking through the windows of the Bank, you can see that the counters and the flooring are once again of Italian Travertine.

There could be no stronger contrast to the Allied Arab Bank than the branch of **Barclays Bank** next door (**17**). Built in 1886, this is the epitome of the Italianate style as realised by Victorian architects, referred to as 'Veneto-Byzantine' by Pevsner. The walls and the elaborate window arcading are in Portland Stone, to which are added rounded shafts and pillars of highly polished pink Peterhead Granite as a striking contrast both of colour and of texture. As a 'red' granite Peterhead is much paler than Shap or Mountsorrel, and infinitely paler than most Scandinavian 'reds' which we see in London. Set against newly cleaned Portland Stone in Cannon Street, the result is

quite elegant, the more so on account of the building which follows to the east (Nos. 106–109 Cannon Street). Here, in **The London Stone Inn** (**18**) we have yet another red granite, the brownish-red Imperial Mahogany Granite from North Dakota. As was the case with the red granite of Norton Warburg and Mecca (**12** above), the swirling patterns of the minerals, the pink veins and the lines of dark inclusions demonstrate that this rock has undergone some measure of alteration or metamorphism, just short of the point where it would have to be called 'gneiss' rather than 'granite'. A similar history of change is evident in the pale buff limestone which lines the interior walls, the fossiliferous Italian Perlato Marble, but the changes here are rather the effect of pressure-solution of the lime mud as it hardened into brittle crystalline limestone than any form of heating or deformation.

Across Oxford Court, a short alley which leads to what was once the graveyard of St Swithun's Church, **London Stone House** (**19**) is so-named because the enigmatic London Stone is embedded into its south wall at pavement level. In the book 'The Stones of London', Elsden and Howe offer the opinion that London Stone may have been a Roman Milestone, which would be a very modest origin for something

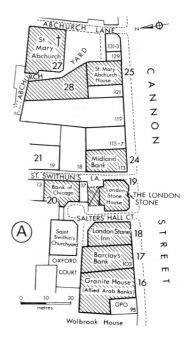

which seems to have acquired a range of myths and legends through its history. In its present protective cage and with its grime-covering it is impossible to offer any useful comment as to whether it is 'ragstone' or something more exotic. Otherwise, this building offers two features of geological interest which we can work out on the pavement of Cannon Street. First, there is the wall which truncates the corner to Oxford Court. This is faced with large slabs of strongly-veined green serpentinite seen earlier in this walk in relatively small surface areas, but here in masses so large that the rock character can be appreciated more fully. Clearly, the original rock has been physically broken down into fragments which are now re-cemented by the ramifying veins, slightly displaced from their original alignments. More profoundly, the original minerals of the sundered rock, whether they were once olivine or pyroxene, have been altered to the end-product chlorite and ores of predominantly green or purple hues which in turn give the rich colouring to this stone. As usual, stone-fitters have used their skill in cutting slabs from solid blocks of serpentinite, opening them like the pages of a book and setting the slabs edge-to-edge have produced mirror-image diamond patterns in this wall surface.

The second rock type of this building is a buff-coloured limestone which at first glance might have been thought to be an artificial stone or even a fine-grained 'concrete'. Closer study will reveal the presence of fossils scattered throughout the entire rock, shell debris which has been broken down to a degree that none of the shells are identifiable beyond the fact that they were probably bivalves. Like the well-known Nabresina Marble from the hills above Trieste the rock here is a Mesozoic limestone of a quality deserving the name 'marble', but its precise provenance is unknown.

Having now reached St Swithin's Lane it is worthwhile diverting from our Cannon Street route to see two new rock types, and a piece of very neat adaptation of an older building to a modern use. Taking the last first, the **American National Bank of Chicago** (**20**) occupies a Victorian building of 1888 (No. 15, St Swithin's Lane) with some very solid facings of pink Peterhead Granite flanking the entrance and extending to the deep rounded arches to the windows to first floor level. In modern renovation, these very tall windows have been reduced by inserts of new stone which turns out to be the dark grey Rustenberg Bon Accord Gabbro once again. The combination of these two stones and the colour contrast achieved, are the success story of this recent adaption of an older building without breaking the harmony of this narrow street of commercial premises. On the opposite side of the lane, Nos. 19–20, **Savill's**, is an office of the same period (**21**), solidly built of red Swedish Granite. Which of the many varieties is not clear. Suffice to say that there are a number of possible sources for such strong, blood-red granites from Central and Southern Sweden, but one of the specific problems of identification here is the loss of surface and the white smear effect which either weathering or stone cleaning may have provoked.

Further up the lane, St Swithin's House is a large, rather featureless block of the 1950's, set back some distance from the line of the street. Beyond its entrance gates on the same side of the lane, is a sequence of modern buildings with more character and with the bonus of interesting natural stones. The first of these comes in No. 10, a newly-added wing to **New Court** (**22**), where we find vertical panels of a silver-grey granite which is Italian Montorfano Granite from the country west of Lake Maggiore in the southern Alps. As a very pale grey granite, Montorfano is recognisable on account of the greenish tinge to its feldspars— the result of a weathering process which has seen their breakdown through a process of kaolinisation from their original alumino-silicate composition. Elsewhere in London, this same granite has been extensively used in the Mermaid Theatre complex of buildings at Puddledock, Blackfriars (1980). Next door to No. 10, New Court itself, the headquarters of **Rothschild's** (**23**) was completed between 1964–65 by Fitzroy, Robinson and Partners. Set back from the Lane beyond a covered entrance courtyard, this building has facings of dark grey Rustenberg Bon Accord Gabbro which offer further opportunity to study the textural variations within this very attractive building stone. In colour, it can range from grey to almost dense black uniformity, with occasional patches or vein-pods of lighter feldspathic material. Unlike other 'Black Granites', it never stands the risk of being taken for plastic or artificial stone, but always smacks of the 'real thing', and good of its kind.

Retracing our steps back to Cannon Street a word must be said about the splendidly Victorian **Midland Bank (24)**, No. 113 Cannon Street. Recently cleaned, the Bank demonstrates the excellent qualities of Portland Stone in its wall stone, the rich Corinthian capitals to its columns and the elaborate roof-level cornice. What probably will stick in

Midland Bank, 113 Cannon Street.

the mind must be the rams' heads and rich foliage frieze at ground level picked out in green paint. Once again, as in Barclays Bank closeby, highly polished columns of pink Peterhead Granite set off the pale colour of the frontage to good effect.

As it happens, the Bank forms the commencement of a whole sequence of buildings on the north side of Cannon Street (Nos. 113–133) which together make up a valuable townscape of varied styles. Contrasting materials, several different functions and yet at the same time forming a cohesive unity, unbroken by any out-of-character modern development. The preservation of such sequences, as far as is possible, was one of the prime objectives of the *Save the City* campaign of 1976 (Lloyd, 1976). Of the sequence, Nos.

115–117, built by the architect J. L. Holmes in 1875, are of Portland Stone and like the Banks described earlier they have rounded columns of pink Peterhead Granite flanking the windows at all three floors combined with well-formed string courses in the same granite. The simplicity of the three floors breaks down at the fourth, which is a riot of swags, cornucopias and cascades of fruit, all in Portland Stone. Elaborate Gothic detail continues in the form of **St Mary Abchurch House** which follows (**25**, Nos. 123–127, Cannon Street). Designed by Huntley Gordon, this very Victorian Building is of terracotta, a material which allowed the moulding of the quite elaborate decorative detail which drips from this frontage (note the cherubs at roof level). As cleaned and resurfaced, the rich red colour of this twinned frontage catches both the eye and the sunlight in any views along Cannon Street to good effect. The building next door, with Harlequin Records at Street level, continues the architectural variety of this sequence with strongly 'Art Nouveau' details, albeit that it was built in 1899. Predominantly of yellowed Portland Stone combined with red brick, the 'Art Nouveau' details are some rather-low relief stylised tree motifs aligned across the bowed front of the building and at roof level, where they are associated with the clear evidence of date '1899'. No. 133 next door is also dated (1921) and in some ways tries to repeat some of the simplicity of line of its neighbour in grey and grimy Portland Stone. This brings us to Abchurch Lane, where, on the south side of the street, almost as a foil to the restless surfaces of the other side, stands the **Banco de Bilbao (26)** renovated and refaced in 1980, simple and white in Portland Stone.

Once again, there are grounds for leaving the line of Cannon Street and exploring Abchurch Lane for a short distance, if only to find a place to sit and rest for a while. This we can find in what was once the churchyard of **St Mary Abchurch (27)**, a Wren church of dull-red brick with stone dressings and a very Dutch spire capping its steeple. The churchyard is an irregular wedge-shaped area, squeezed by the backward extension of Nos. 123–127, Cannon Street and offices constricting the narrow alley of Abchurch Yard. The whole area is

Churchyard of St Mary Abchurch.

cobbled and paved, with decorative roundels set out in grey Purbeck Limestone (the non-fossiliferous variety from the Swanage cliff tops), grey-blue slate (? from North Wales) and dull-red Mountsorrel Granite. Facing on to the churchyard, and alongside the red terracotta continuation of Abchurch House seen earlier from its Cannon Street frontage, we can take in the former Banco Totta & Acores (**28**), a combination of brick and a yellowish coloured limestone. This is a form of Bath Stone, an orange-brown oolitic limestone from the middle Jurassic rocks of the Cotswold Avon Valley, large quantities of which were quarried and mined in the mid-19th century to meet the boom in growth of all the towns and cities of industrial Britain. Possibly it was the pressure to supply large quantities of stone with insufficient initial preparation, as much as the ill-effects of polluted city air which was the downfall of Bath Stone in some London buildings. As it happens, this Bank shows quite well-preserved surfaces of an even grained oolite variety.

Returning to Cannon Street, set back some distance from the main line of the road is the modern tower complex, Nos. 110–114, **The Midland Bank International** (**29**), occupying most of the space between Laurence Pountney Lane and Martin Lane and almost reaching Lower Thames Street in the direction of the river, downslope. The sheer size of the towers and the bulk of the ground plan create one lasting impression, but equally striking must be the stonework which is of a deep colour, unrelieved by any touches of light—even the glass is brown-tinted. The stone in question is sometimes called Carnation Red Granite, sometimes Imperial Red Granite; what is not in doubt is that the rock comes from Sweden and that it is virtually the same stone which we saw earlier on this walk in Cannon Street (stop **12**). Here again, in the

Detail of Swedish Imperial Red Granite (Midland Bank International).

Midland Bank, we can see the crushed feldspar crystals as distinct cores around which the rest of the rock appears to 'flow' creating a version of what is termed 'augen-structure' (from the German, comparing the cores to eyes), a well-known metamorphic texture of gneisses. Within the foyer of the building the well surfaces about the lift shafts are lined with an attractive white marble, which from the delicate green veining, is thought to be Italian Botticino Marble.

Coutts Bank, 143 Cannon Street; quarter-matched marble panel.

On the opposite side of Cannon Street, No. 143 is another square-framed block on the 1950's, rendered yet more featureless by the blind-eyed mirror glass of the windows. At street level the entrance to **Coutts & Company (30)** is a focus of interest on account of the quarter-matched panels of dark-veined Paonazzetto Marble which have been skilfully aligned to produce a series of elongate diamond outlines. It is difficult to explain sensibly and simply the causes of veining in marble other than to say that often it seems that the process of recrystallisation of the original limestone, produces a form of segregation of the impurities (mainly clay minerals) from the pure calcium carbonate which makes up the greater part of the rock. What impurities there are, clay minerals or included grains, are instrumental in creating the body colour, if any, of the marble. Otherwise, they form the veins which ramify throughout the rock and give it its 'figure'.

Across Nicholas Lane was the 1930's bulk of **Phoenix House (31)** extending as a corner site around into King William Street. Recently (1981—82) the building was renovated as headquarters for Phoenix Assurance, in the course of which, its original combination of granite and Portland Stone has been replaced by two new granites. The largest areas are faced with pale Sardinian Grey Granite, but in the faces to Nicholas Lane and the corner to Cannon Street the darker horizontals are of Norwegian Blaubrun Granite. The 'brownness' stems from biotite mica, the 'blueness' from strained quartz. If you view the slabs from Cannon Street, the almost metamorphic foliation is further evidence of strain.

The last building of Cannon Street, No. 120, **Candlewick House (32)** facing on to the junction with King William and Gracechurch Street,

Phoenix House, Cannon Street; Blaubrun Granite and Sardinian Grey Granite

shows large surfaces at street level of an orange-buff travertine. Darker than the usual Italian travertine from Tivoli Quarries near Rome, the colour here is strengthened by the tone of the filling material which has been used to 'stop' the natural cavities within the original rock. At one time, almost all of the travertine used in building came from the one source in Italy but now, with the growing popularity of the material, alternative sources in Spain, Germany and Portugal can provide travertines with a wider range of colours and textures. All tend to be relatively young geologically speaking from either Tertiary or Pleistocene sequences.

At the same corner, but further round towards the approach to London Bridge, stands **The Moscow Narodny Bank (33)**, a late 1950's building in which we return to a mixture of different rock types and polychrome effects. Most striking of these may be the pillars to the entrance and the banking hall which are clad in the black and gold Portoro Marble from the Siena region of the Apennines. The body of the rock is a dense black limestone through which there run wide veins of orange-yellow dolomitic material and within which are caught up small fragments of the same black limestone. Viewing these surfaces one gains a distinct impression of the dynamic break-up of rock which has gone on in the course of formation of this true marble. Other marbles, one white with faint blue veins, the other a slate-blue with faint white veins, form a chequer-board tiling at the other end of the banking hall. Standing back from the Bank, the narrow horizontal panels between the floors are of a grey granite of unknown provenance (? Dalbeattie) but difficult to determine from street level, other than to note its darker colour and finer texture than normal granites.

From the front of the Moscow Narodny Bank, it is very difficult to make direct progress eastwards because of the barriers which protect the pedestrians from the steady traffic flow from London Bridge into the City. Thus marooned on the west side pavement, we might do well to take stock of the buildings around us. To the south, the eye is caught by the downsweep of the street to the viaduct which bridges across Lower Thames Street, beyond which follows the broad

openness of the new bridge. The surviving South Bank wharves and the lumpen redevelopment of Southwark are framed in this view by the impressive bulk of **Adelaide House (34)** to the left and the upper storeys of **Fishmongers Hall (35)** to the right—buildings very contrasted in styles and in their relationship to the level of the new London Bridge. Adelaide House, for example, seems to dominate the bridge approach as if intended for the situation of the 1960's, whereas it was actually built in 1925 by Burnet & Tait when the scene was quite different, the area being a conglomeration of functioning wharehouses and riverside wharves lining Lower Thames Street. In contrast to this confusion, the lines of this major office block are impressively simple and clean, the solid Portland Stone walling being relieved by restrained ornament and only the Egyptian-like columns to the entrance. What we see of Fishmongers Hall is only the uppermost levels of a thoroughly classical building of the early 19th century, matching in style and stone Somerset House with touches of British Museum (Bloomsbury, not South Kensington). To see the building in its true perspective, it is necessary to take the new riverside walk from Lower Thames street, when, after the brutalism of the multi-storey car parks, the columnate and pedimented frontage of the Hall to the river takes on an obvious attraction.

King William Street House and Arthur Street from The Monument.

Guardian Royal Exchange Building and King William Street from The Monument.

In the past year (1983), a very striking new building, **King William Street House** (**36**) has filled the triangular space between London Bridge and the descending curve of Arthur Street. To meet this change of height and irregular space, the solution has been to design a tower with octagon form, rising from a base platform faced in rough-riven Sardinian Beige Granite. The building is further diversified by the introduction of knobbly surfaces of well-rounded sea ballast (mostly flint cobbles) where otherwise there might have been uneven paving of York Stone. The best surfaces for study are to be found in the rampart-like inclined flanks which face on to Arthur Street, especially with the advantage of afternoon sunlight.

Looking to the north from our same pavement viewpoint, the massive offices of **The Guardian Royal Exchange Insurance Company** (**37**) are a cliff of yellowed Portland Stone, based by axe-dressed grey granite (probably Cornish), effectively splitting traffic flow into the City either along King William Street or Gracechurch Street. Compared with Adelaide House of the same period, this building seems fussy with detail and not improved by the blankness of the mirror glass to all the windows. Directly facing us on the opposite corner, we can find greater geological interest in **Monument Station Buildings** (**38**), a Victorian series of offices and shop fronts faced with deeply moulded pillars

and arches in a Peterhead Granite of a darker tone of red than is normal. There are two points to note, the first being the series of inclusions of dark schist within the granite which can be seen particularly to the left of the main entrance to the Buildings and in the stonework of The Monument Tavern. The dark schist is speckled with small growths of feldspar within its mass, and its margins corroded into a rounded outline by the fusion and assimilation which have taken place between the granite melt and the included fragment. The second point is merely an observation on the care of buildings. Polished surfaces of the best granites can deteriorate over the years, becoming flat and dull in appearance; washing and cleaning of stone is as much a necessity as it is for windows, and can 'save' a surface. Here in Monument Station Building the surfaces have been well-maintained and look splendid for those pains.

If we follow round into Fish Street Hill, this short cobbled lane brings us directly to **The Monument** (**39**), sited close to the famous Bakery in Pudding Lane and recorded as the starting point for the Great Fire of 1666. Appropriately, The Monument is of Portland Stone, in the sense that the disaster which resulted in the destruction of some ninety City churches also allowed the reconstruction of at least fifty of them in the following forty years in this very same building stone. Equally

The Monument.

appropriate was the involvement of Robert Hooke in the design of The Monument, for it reminds us that Chirstopher Wren had the assistance of a large team of other architects in his rebuilding work, including Hooke and Hawksmoor. The Monument involves many of the features of a Roman Triumphal Column—a massive Ionic Shaft rising from a tall, squared base, but for the record, at 61 m, it is almost twice the height of Trajan's Column in Rome. Visualising the crisp cornices and sharp angles of the original structure, we can quickly appreciate the extent of weathering which has reduced the good-quality limestone in the space of some 250 years—notice for example the pockmarks produced by rain drip on to the horizontal surfaces of the base. As is usual for Portland Stone, the loss of surface has resulted in the emergence of fragments of fossil shell as tougher elements within the limestone, these now standing out proud from what was originally a smooth ashlar surface finish.

The Monument stands in a small cobbled square which is on the fringe of the extensive redevelopment of the Billingsgate and Monument Street areas. To the north, at the foot of Fish Street Hill, is **Lloyds Bank (40)**, a modern building built in 1967, employing Larvikite as cladding but with a matt-surfaced finish in contrast to the customary high surface polish seen earlier in Bucklersbury House (**11** above). Even with this treatment the large feldspar crystals can be made out in low incident light and the rock retains a measure of the usual metallic lustre. As if to counterbalance the modern with something different, to the south of The Monument facing Lloyds Bank is **Monument House (41)**, an office building of rather crumbling Bath Stone enhanced by columns of pink Peterhead Granite about the entrance and at first floor level. Perhaps only a geologist would seek its preservation, if only for sight of Bath Stone slightly decayed, but like other buildings of the late-Victorian period we see a carefree confusion of architectural details worked out in a wide range of natural and artificial materials typical for that period of time.

Moving down Monument Street, we come to **Faryners House (42)**,

Cheapside roof levels from The Monument.

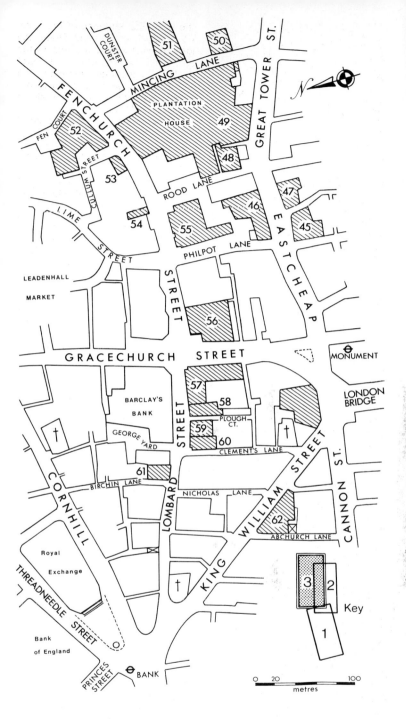

designed by Seiferts for Lloyds Bank in 1971, a building in which we see the building mode of the 70's as clearly as we saw that for 1870 in Monument House. Here the materials are concrete, pre-cast panels and touches of natural stone, with the pre-cast panels most prominent Dusty and dull, the rock involved could be almost anything, but close to the pavement on the north side, it seems to be grey granite. In the skin to the great Y-form struts which brace the angles to the building, however, the white flake pebble dash panels are of burnt flint, the crazed surface to the chips telling of the heat treatment of the silica masses. Natural stone comes into the fabric of Faryners House in the entrance from Monument Street where there are broad surfaces of grey-black Rustenberg Bon Accord Gabbro.

In years to come, the protracted development of the site of the Coal Exchange (a scheduled building sadly lost some years ago) and of Billingsgate Market, will continue to be discussed, much as the still-longer debate over the loss of the Euston Arch. Here, close to the Monument, there now stands on what was the Coal Exchange site, **The Trade Development Bank** and **Peninsular House**, a massive block of highly polished, deep red Finnish Granite. The stone is another example of a rock which has been partially crushed by later crustal movements— that fact registered by the streaking out of the minerals, particularly the feldspars. What we also see are polished and a rough textured versions of the same stone in different parts of the building complex. The Billingsgate site is still in early stage of redevelopment (1983) and it is not certain yet what it may add to the geology of the area.

For our part, however, we profit by turning northwards up St Botolph's Lane and back towards Eastcheap. On the right hand side of the lane, there is stone to note in the renovated premises of **Derek Bryan** Insurance Brokers (**43**). This was a simple brick-built office which has been enhanced at ground floor level with panels of green Lake District Slate, a rock previously seen at a distance in Bucklersbury House above Budge Row. At closer quarters it can be seen that the colour banding corresponds to different grain size in the sediment and that some of the band contacts are quite irregular. This is evidence of erosion at the time of sedimentation, reminding us that these volcanic ashes were waterlain. As we move on into Botolph Alley, it is perhaps timely to draw attention to bricks and brickwork in this area of the City. Victorian commercial buildings in these narrow streets and lanes have often become dulled and begrimed over the years, but beneath the dirt there can be sound brick of a variety of colours and textures other than the flat biscuit colour of the London Stock. In Botolph Lane and the nearby St Mary's Hill we have a chance to see the effect which can be achieved by cleaning and resurfacing by mild brushing without breaking the outer protective skin of the brick. We can also appreciate how Victorian builders used bricks which were moulded and cut to a specific shape to achieve a decorative pattern such as a date or a dedication panel, an ornamental string-course or an attached pilaster to a wall surface. Thus, in St Botolph's Lane, the rich red brick of No. 39 is in marked contrast to the strong yellow brick of the office next door bridging the arch-entrance to Botolph Alley. Such contrasts certainly brighten up the otherwise dark narrow lanes of this quarter of the City.

Botolph Alley leads us into Lovat Lane and the west front of the Wren church of **St Mary-at-Hill** (**44**), a building very much confined in shape by the surrounding buildings so that it has no exterior to remember, but as if to make up, an interior which is unexpectedly fine. The surrounding area is of high priority in the conservation of the City, and for that reason is undergoing extensive refurbishing at an appropriate level. From it, our course takes us back to Eastcheap, where, at the head of Lovat Lane, **The Banco di Roma** (**45**) offers broad surfaces of a dark-grey granite flecked with stumpy white feldspars spaced evenly through the entire rock. This is the Ulster Bessbrook Granite from Armagh, a rock closely similar in colour to Rubislaw Granite from Aberdeen, but distinguished from it by its white feldspars and its lack of dark schist inclusions. For good measure, at the curved corner surface to the Bank there are inserts of pink Peterhead Granite facing on to Eastcheap.

From this point on the south side of the main thoroughfare, we face a group of buildings on the north side, **Nos. 23–39, Eastcheap** (**46**), which repeat the effect seen earlier in Cannon Street. In close proximity we have a sequence of Victorian offices and shops, varied and contrasted in styles and materials, which have somehow managed to survive unchanged and which, if they continue unaltered, can give a vital lift to this broad City street. Beginning at the foot of Philpot Lane, we have the what was The Kardomah Cafe (1893) introduces a range of colour-contrasting igneous rocks in the solid columns of the entrance. The columns themselves are of polished grey-blue Larvikite seated on squared bases which combine dark grey Rubislaw Granite (the tops and bottoms) and pink Peterhead Granite (the main middle section to the column base). No. 31, The Lautrec Restaurant, is strictly non-geological at ground level, but at first floor has a composite window tracery which demonstrates how Victorian builders expressed an enthusiasm for brick-work. This is a building of a pale yellow brick, but the broad arches of the windows are picked out in bricks of different colours to good effect. What has gone before as examples of Victorian Gothic must immediately be overshadowed by what follows in the total effect of Nos. 33–35, a

Nos. 23–29 Eastcheap in multicolour brick.

Venetian-Gothic No. 23, built in 1862 as a warehouse for a spice merchant by the architect John Young. The records tell us that at one time he worked for Decimus Burton, in which case the exuberant use of coloured brick in the window surrounds and the roof level cornice crowded with animal heads, might be seen as a release of the pent-up restraints of earlier years. Nos. 27-29 next door make up the next unit in the sequence, a building of red brick with painted-over stone dressings, rising to a tall Dutch-style gable flanked by curving stone volutes. At street level the frontage to

Nos, 33–35 Eastcheap.

building which it is difficult to appreciate was originally designed as a warehouse for a Wine and Vinegar merchant by the architect R. L. Roumieu (1868). More like an attenuated Keble College, the building is of a deep red brick with diaper work picked out in black. The whole effect is set off by stone dressings which we are told were of Tisbury Stone, although this is a detail hidden by the present overpainting which adds lustre to the whole street at this point. Were it seen, Tisbury Stone, which is a distant relation of Portland Stone extended into Wiltshire would have a slightly greenish cast derived from the grains of the mineral glauconite which speckle the creamy coloured limestone.

Almost any building would seem quiet by comparison with what has just gone before, but Nos. 37–39, Eastcheap are a unit of very simple lines, Portland Stone throughout, with large windows framed by slender columns of Red Sandstone (probably New Red Sandstone from the Midlands).

Compared with the restless activity and rapid changes of style of the north pavement the entire south side at this point is occupied by the solid mass of **Peek House** (47), a building which incorporates a Bank, Offices and City Chambers extending from Lovat Lane to St Mary Hill as a single unit. Overall, the building shows design details borrowed from Egyptian architecture or rather motifs which popularly represented Egypt to the Victorian mind. These come out most strongly in the decorative frieze to the Midland Bank at the head of Lovat Lane in the camel trains sculpted in low relief in yellowed Portland Stone. At pavement level, Peak House shows axe-dressed grey granite, which, when polished in the entrance surrounds, proves to be either Rubislaw Granite once again or possibly the darker Ben Cruachan from Argyllshire.

Rood Lane, the Wren church of **St Margaret Pattens** (48) and a group of surviving Georgian town houses, provide a quiet back-water in Eastcheap before the widened street is dominated by **Plantation House** (49), one of the most substantial

Plantation House, Eastcheap.

building complexes of the City, extending as it does from Eastcheap to Mincing Lane, north to Fenchurch Street and west as far as Rood Lane to complete the square. Built between 1934 and 1937 to a design by A. W. Moore, Plantation House maintains a massive Imperial style of architecture, with grand entrances to all fronts, flanked by giant columns all in solid Portland Stone upon a base of grey Cornish Granite. At first floor level facing on to Mincing Lane and Fenchurch Street, the building is encircled by a heavy frieze of tropical fruits and seeds broken by coats of arms of former colonial territories, all of which combines to tell of the original associations of the building with the trade in tea and spices. Nowadays there are many different functions for the suites of offices of this mammoth building of the late-30's, offices interconnected by broad corridors lined and paved in rich antique marble. Taking the wings facing on to Eastcheap, the interesting detail of Plantation House must be the base course which is in large feldspar Lamorna Granite from Cornwall.

Turning up Mincing Lane to begin retracing our steps towards the Bank notice the dark grey Rubislaw Granite in the refaced **United Bank** (50). Then, in the succeeding building on the same side of the lane, study the grey stone which faces the pillars fronting **Colonial House** (51), a 1956 building slightly set back from the line of Mincing Lane. At first, this rock could seem featureless, but careful scrutiny will detect small white round 'inclusions'; these are crinoid ossicles, to which we can add a rarer cone-shaped coral all of which goes to prove that here we have panels of Carboniferous Limestone fitted together to form these hollow pillars (tap them and you will get a ringing sound which tells that they are not solid through-and-through). There should be fewer problems in identifying the Larvikite panels which flank the northern entrance to Colonial House.

From this point, it is worth looking across to Plantation House on the opposite side of the lane, to take in the massive bronze doors and the flanking decoration of rubber leaves, coffee plants, tea, and spices, all carved in Portland Stone in strong relief. From here too, we can take in the form of **Fountain House** (52) at the head of the Lane and on the north side of Fenchurch Street. This was a building completed in 1957 by W. H. Rodgers, and is recorded as being the first transfer to London of the building style of Lever House, New York, a low horizontal block from which springs a slender, vertical tower, a pattern widely copied subsequently (Pevsner, 1962).

A steel-framed building with considerable surface area taken up by windows, geological interest is confined to ground floor level and the area about the entrances. These include buff-coloured Italian travertine and pale blue Larvikite in the main building, and panels of green Serpentinite in the Midland Bank occupying the corner site facing Cullum Street.

On the opposite corner of Cullum Street, **Underwoods** the Chemist (**53**) shows a modernised frontage which combines the two rough textured rock types currently used in the City, Italian Travertine as just seen in Fountain House, linked with Portland Roach. The Roach surfaces are particularly good for seeing examples of the tall-spired gastropod *Procerithium* (the 'Portland Screw') and the cauliflower clusters which are calcareous algal colonies which are one of the factors which allow us to recognise the warm sub-tropical character of Portland times. Fossil algae are also prominent in the rich brown polished surfaces of the doorway to Nos. 141–142, Fenchurch Street next door, but the provenance is unknown for this decorative rock.

If we now slip down Rood Lane, we are in a position to appreciate a piece of modern renovation of older Victorian premises on the north side of Fenchurch Street. Here again we have a series of three buildings (**54**) which together make up a period sequence in the midst of much younger architecture. The first is a building of Portland Stone of a relatively simple style and with a smooth surface finish. This has been cleaned to a flat whiteness which sets off the offices on either side. At street level, the entrance has been deepened into a foyer which is lined with the buff coloured Perlato Marble from Italy. Above, each floor has varied design touches; each window a different tracery, fronted by a bulging balcony in stone. At first and fourth floors there are columns of Peterhead Granite, with spheres of the same red rock deep-set into the walling below the balconies. The

Nos. 144–53 Fenchurch Street; Victorian frontages modernised.

building of the same period next door (above the premises of **Simon Paul**) is completely fronted by continuous panels of brown glass, totally concealing the stonework, but continuously reflecting the steeple of St Margaret Pattens behind us at the foot of Rood Lane. The side-by-side contrast, and the dramatic reflection, are a touch of magic at this point in Fenchurch Street completed by the fiery red terracota of the third building, No. 153, **Aspreys** (dated 1880). The Kleinwort Benson Tower with its main entrance to Fenchurch Street, has a ground floor lined with some excellent surfaces of Devonian age Torquay Marble (**55**). This was the rock type simulated in the plastic panels of Drake House, Dowgate Hill (stop **13** above), and attempt at deception which is made to look very cheap when we see the real thing here in the staircase walling for example. This British marble was originally a dark coloured muddy limestone, crowded with fossil corals and other shells, which was later deformed and altered to the condition of a true marble. Other than the fossils mentioned, the attractive patterning of the rock stems from the blood red veins which criss-cross its cut surfaces, giving it an antique marble air.

Continuing westwards, the buildings of Fenchurch Street offer little until we reach the junction with Gracechurch Street and come upon the large screen-wall which once formed the backdrop to the sculpture 'Spirit of Enterprise'. Here we have a unique stone in the shape of Epigneiss or Shangdong Greenstone from Andeer in southern Switzerland. The rock is quarried in the uppermost reaches of the Rhine Valley, just north of the San Bernadino Pass, where there are exposed Alpine-core rocks of a high metamorphic grade. The greenstone shows augen texture once again, the cores or augen being either crushed quartzes or streaked-out feldspars, all set in a swirling wreath of chloritic material. A little weather-stained, this wall should be a place of pilgrimage for any structural geologist wishing to see a rock which comes from the roots of a mountain chain. (**56**).

Detail of the mouldings to the entrance, Barclays Bank, Lombard Street.

Barclays Banks, Gracechurch-Lombard Street intersection.

Barclays Bank, Gracechurch Street opposite (**57**) was refurbished in 1981 to join up with the elegant Victorian Bank at the corner of Lombard Street. It has simple lines by comparison, and some geological additions to the basic Portland Stone of the original building. The dark grey-black polished slabs are South African Eagle Granite (in fact it is a Gabbro), slightly bronzy in colourcast compared with the now-familiar Rustenberg, but probably from the same Bushveld Complex. As a rock, there is a smaller proportion of feldspar and a corresponding increase of the darker minerals, hence the blacker tone overall. In contrast

to this dark rock, the deep arches to the windows of the Bank are picked out with a pure white marble, figured with only faint blue-grey veins. It is from Carrara. Turning now to the ornate Italianate older Bank at the corner, this was a building of the Francis Brothers of 1868, which matches in its elegant detail their other Bank in Cornhill (now Banco del Lavoro). Recently cleaned by washing and brushing treatments, again we have demonstrated the excellence of Portland Stone for sculptural detail, particularly the heavy roof cornices. Looking at the Bank from Lombard Street, the ornament at ground floor level includes vine-leaves and grape clusters in high relief. Geologists will note more especially some very naturalistic scallop shells alternating with the eagles in the capitals to the attached pillars. Hardly a square inch of surface is without some decoration, with something new to see at each visit it seems.

Next door, **The Northern Trust Bank of Chicago** (**58**) in normal company would have seemed quite ornate in Portland Stone with panels of grey Kemnay Granite at ground level and about the entrance. Like the other Chicago Bank in Swithin's Lane, this is a late-19th century building which has been skilfully modernised while retaining most of its original proportions and details including the bulgy brass number plate (No. 38).

Beyond Plough Court, brilliant blue Larvikite returns in the **Lombard Central Bank (59)**, with contrasting black Rustenberg Bon Accord Gabbro at pavement level. The same Larvikite figures prominently in the modernised frontage of **The Clydesdale Bank (60)**, but coming to the entrance close to the head of Clement's Lane we come upon another geological surprise in the form of the pink-and-white brecciated marble which forms the tall vertical screen set back and at an angle to the street. This is Norwegian Rose Marble from a belt of deformed limestones of Palaeozoic age within the Caledonide Mountains of Norway. Surfaces such as those offered here allow a much fuller appreciation of the textures of such deformed rocks, their fracture and recrystallisation under stress.

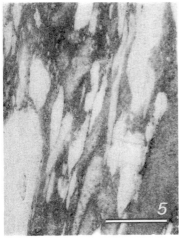

Detail of Norwegian Rose Marble, Clydesdale Bank, Lombard Street.

Little can be said of the enormous Barclays Bank building on the north side of Lombard Street, except that it is a massive cliff of very white Portland Stone, with a 2 m base course of fine grained dark dressed grey granite (Dalbeattie Granite?). The same finish equally conceals the character of the granite which makes up ground and first floors of the refitted Royal Bank of Scotland at the top of Clement's Lane, but surely it must be Scottish out of sheer patriotism. This is certainly the case with the much more elegant Bank which stands alongside the Wren church of St Edmund the King on the north side of Lombard Street

(61). This was built for **The Royal Bank of Scotland** by John MacVicar Anderson in 1889 with beautifully calculated proportions and a flourish of three contrasting Scottish granites. One was the grey-brown Kemnay Granite from mid-Aberdeenshire; the second was pink Peterhead Granite; the third was the less well-known Ben Cruachan Granite, a dark grey granite from the northern end of Loch Awe in Argyllshire. Granite continues as walling and columns up to first floor levels, above which comes white Portland Stone in the upper storeys. A scheduled building for its architectural merit, this Bank deserves protection for its geology to an equal degree, and will survive the present renovation (1983).

Lombard Street now becomes a Portland Stone canyon, the rear walls of the large Cornhill Banks pressing in to funnel traffic towards the busy junction of The Royal Exchange and Bank. So it profits our search for yet more and different rock types to proceed down either Nicholas or Abchurch Lanes to regain King William Street. Here, solid Edwardian and 1920's Insurance Offices (The Phoenix, and London Life are typical), all in Portland Stone, are offset by **The Banque National de Paris (62)**, designed by Fitzroy, Robinson and Partners and winning a Civic Trust Award in 1979. A striking modern building, its windows are set back from the busy street between projecting buttresses of stone which extend vertically throughout the frontage. The stone used is the orange-buff Sardinian Beige Granite owing its distinctive colouring to the main orthoclase feldspar which makes up almost 45% of the total rock.

Like Cannon Street at the commencement of this walk, King William Street was a thoroughfare cut boldly through the pattern of Lanes which previously dominated this part of the City. To the north and to the south, the truncated Lanes survive, lined by the confining buildings which have been replaced piecemeal over the years and still continuing to be so. King William Street itself effectively focusses attention to the Bank intersection and the association of buildings which surround it in Poultry and Princes Street leading to Moorgate, but these are the subject of another walk.

Threadneedle Street from The Royal Exchange. Foreground, Bank of Nova Scotia; behind, The Stock Exchange; background, The National Westminster Tower.

ROYAL EXCHANGE TO ALDGATE

Our starting point for this walk is the eastern end of The Royal Exchange building, not far from that central focal point of City streets, The Bank of England. Standing at the kerbside in Threadneedle Street, one is strategically placed to take in a panorama of buildings ranging in age over two hundred years of time and over a wide spectrum of architectural taste and practice. In spite of this range we recognise a persistent convention that grand and public buildings are founded upon a base course of granite, overtopped by ashlar finished Portland Stone—the City's inheritance from the rebuilding after The Great Fire of 1666. Most buildings within sight are of a form derived from classical origins, becoming diversified by renaissance touches when we come to Victorian contributions, and more massive in scale when we come to Edwardian and 1930's additions as seen at the foot of Poultry. With a lapse of almost fifty years, we come to the bolder, cleaner lines of modern buildings which also depart from tradition by introducing polished igneous rocks on a large scale. The new Stock Exchange (1975–76) or the Angel Court development (1980) with their beautiful polished granite panels, are excellent examples of this period. Finally, towering above even these modern units, we can see from this same viewpoint, the upper part of the new National Westminster Tower. Two hundred metres of glass and metal rising from a substantial base clad in natural stone, form a 1981 contribution to the fascinating mosaic of City geology which must satisfy the geologist if not the planner or architectural historian.

Starting with what is closest to hand, it is worth mentioning that the present **Royal Exchange (1)**, is actually the third on the site of the Exchange originally established by Thomas Gresham to promote the trading business of the City in 1566. The previous two Exchanges having been destroyed by fire, there was an obvious requirement that the winning design from the competition of 1838 should be a substantial stone building, as well as something architecturally imposing to face up to the nearby Bank of England. In the event, the winning design came from William Tite, a pupil of Sir John Soane, so naturally his Exchange was a wholly classical building with a fully columnate portico facing west, capped by a tympanum which must be among the most richly decorated in London. His style was grandiose and imposing, as was the aim of much Victorian commercial architecture—all aptly summarised by Pevsner in the phrase,

'Purity is thrown to the winds for the sake of richness—a typical sign of the approaching Victorian Age'. (Pevsner, 1962)

Geologically, The Royal Exchange has massive base blocks of granite at pavement level. The blocks are up to 2 m tall and axe-dressed to produce a slightly dull surface effect. Nevertheless, through the flat, matt surface, large white crystals of feldspar can be made out which effectively identify the rock as one of the large feldspar granites from one of the intrusives in Cornwall. Weathering, partly in the form of rising damp, has caused some exfoliation of the rock but if anything this has emphasized the porphyritic texture of the granite as the large feldspars stand out as knotty prominences on the flaked surfaces. Above this massive base, the walls of the Exchange and the massive drum sections of the columns at either end are of Portland Stone from either the Whit- or Base-Bed units of the Dorset quarries, these being the most even-grained and thickest of the several bands which make up the total limestone succession, and those most sought after for good masonry work in building contracts. These are also the grade of stone which is most suitable for sculptural detail such as the column capitals or the appropriate statue to Gresham which stands in a niche high on the north face of the Exchange.

At this point, we can shift our attention to the new **Stock Exchange (2)** as a marked contrast to all we have seen in the Victorian face of City commerce. Rising on the other side of Threadneedle Street this building complex, designed by Llewellyn Davies and Partners (1976), offers some of the largest surface areas of polished granite available at street level in which we can admire the skill of the stonefitters in producing continuous

Granite walling to the Stock Exchange on Threadneedle Street.

panels with almost invisible joins. The same surfaces, thanks to the high surface polish attained, offer us ample opportunity to study mineral textures over areas several metres square from which we can appreciate swirling patterns of movement as the molten material of the granite cooled. This 'flow' is conveyed by the slender lath-form feldspar crystals orienting themselves like iron-filings in a magnetic field. Dark, glassy areas at close quarters are the mineral quartz; feldspars are opaque white or grey; while wisps of black tend to be biotite mica appearing to wrap around clusters of other minerals. Once again, this grey granite is from Cornwall, but this is Hantergan-

tick Granite from a quarter of Bodmin Moor where the granite is even grained and non-porphyrytic. The same rock was recently used in the extension to the Old Bailey and in the new London Bridge. Here in Threadneedle Street, the upper floors of The Stock Exchange become shuttered concrete, producing an unsightly limey downwash—'sic transit gloria mundi'.

Next to The Stock Exchange and directly north of Royal Exchange is **The Bank of Nova Scotia** (3), another modern building involving large surface areas of natural stone throughout its six storeys—stone set off by silvery alloy window surrounds. The stone used here is

Detail of Hantergrantick Granite, from the wall above.

Norwegian Larvikite, of the brilliant electric-blue colour which is the current output of the large quarries on the west shores of Oslo Fjord close to the town of Larvik. The distinctive iridescence of these polished surfaces is the result of light reflection from the large feldspar crystals which make up the greater part of this igneous rock. Being poor in silica, and lacking quartz as a component mineral, it should be termed a syenite rather than a granite. The large plagioclase crystals are often a complex intergrowth of two feldspars, within

tals. The third granite is greyer in colour, although it also has small pink feldspars in its groundmass when we look closely. This is Verde Mergozzo Granite, again from Italy (I am indebted to the architects Millard, Wrighton and Wynn for these precise details from the specifications of 1965). The sheer walls of the office are of Portland Stone, but in contrast to that of The Royal Exchange this particular variety is visibly full of cavities and pitted overall. This surface texture is typical of the variety of Portland Stone known by the quarryman's term

'Black Granite', and Portland Roach, Eagle Star Insurance.

which are caught up grains of magnetite clearly visible against the silvery reflectance of the larger minerals. Larvikite buildings need good sunlight to emphasise the quality of the stone; here in Threadneedle Street and not overshadowed by tall buildings to the south, this Bank often catches the eye.

To the east of us, yet another modern building faces the east front of The Royal Exchange, No. 1 Threadneedle Street, the headquarters of **The Eagle Star Insurance Company** (4). Here we find no fewer than three different igneous rocks combined with larger surface areas of Portland Stone. At the base is a highly polished, dense black rock, which in the stone trade would be termed 'Black Granite'.

In this particular case, the stone came from Morocco. Turning to the window surrounds of the building, the salmon-pink granite is known as Granito Rosa and is from Italy, its pink colour stemming from the larger orthoclase feldspar crys-

Roach. The cavities are created by the solution of the fossil shell content by groundwaters. It is clearly evident from the close spaced casts of bivalves, gastropods and the cauliflower-like clumps of calcareous algae which we can see on these surfaces that Roach must have been a much shellier limestone than either Whit- or Base-Bed Portland. We can also see here in the sheer walls of the Eagle Star building the unsightly effect of limewash from mortars and Portland Stone itself where the architect has created sheer wall surfaces, unbroken by string courses or ledges, worse still, has introduced into the fabric of the building black polished alabs liable to show every trace of downwash.

Directly in front of us on the paved walk, stands the statue to **William Peabody** on a plinth of a distinctive dull red granite flecked with touches of green. While it is distinctive in its colour and texture, its identity as Trowelsworthy Granite, a Dartmoor Granite unusual in its red colour, was only determined by reference to the very large collection of building stones which is part of the collection of The Geological Museum of the Institute of Geological Sciences in Exhibition Road, South Kensington. This remains an unrivalled reference source on such questions. Peabody himself deserves comment as being the Boston philanthropist who did much in the mid-19th century to house the poorer working people of London by providing blocks of flats at low rents in the boroughs of inner London—the well-known Peabody Buildings of Clerkenwell, Aldgate and Stepney.

Nearby is one of the two fountains mentioned by Professor Pevsner with approval in his 'Buildings of England' volume dealing with London, his judgement can be reinforced on geological grounds. This fountain is a typical Victorian confection; the pedestal is again of Trowelsworthy with its dull red hue, but the flanking basins and other details are of a grey-brown granite with spectacularly large crystals of orthoclase feldspar reminiscent of those seen in the granite base to The Royal Exchange. The precise source of this elegant granite is not known, but it is safe to say that it is an excellent example of a porphyritic texture, and undoubtedly came from

Cornwall. There are two further points to note; first, the large feldspars often show evidence of periods of growth through ghostly outlines picked out by small grain-inclusions; secondly, there is often a detectable parallel orientation between the elongate crystals which gives a sense of flow in a semi-fluid granite melt. Despite this impression, growth may have been in solid-state.

Statue to Julius Reuter, Royal Exchange Buildings.

Midway along the paved walk behind the Exchange there is the monument to **Reuter**, founder of the Press Agency, an unusual monument in that the head and shoulders emerge from the top of a rough-hewn upright plinth of fine-grained grey granite after the style of Karl Marx in Highgate Cemetery. Equally unusual is the long inscription on the plinth executed in letters which are in relief rather than the customary incised engraved form. The source of the granite is unknown, but it bears a strong resemblance to any small-feldspar Bodmin Moor Granite.

Royal Exchange Building in front of us (**5**), is solidly of Portland Stone of the Whit- or Base-Bed grade. Built in 1907–10, it has recently been cleaned by sand-blasting and water spray techniques and survives slightly pock-marked. As an Edwardian building, it has a style which a palaeontologist would say had evolved from a Victorian ancestor; not so much Italian Renaissance as Empire Commercial, but the stone is attractive.

Fountain of granites from South West England, north end of the pavement, Royal Exchange Buildings.

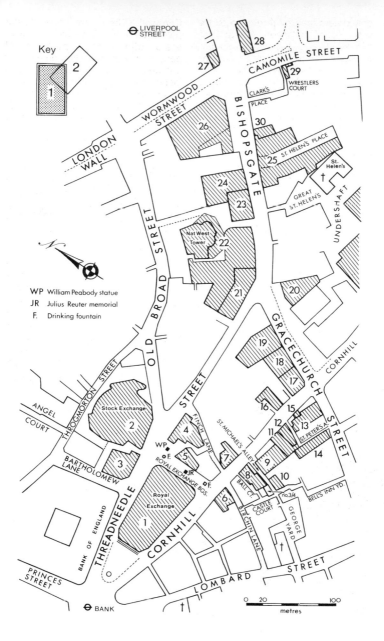

Key

2

1

LIVERPOOL STREET

28

CAMOMILE STREET

27

29

CLARK'S PLACE

WRESTLERS COURT

WORMWOOD STREET

26

30

ST. HELEN'S PLACE

25

St. Helen's

LONDON WALL

BISHOPSGATE

24

GREAT ST. HELEN'S

23

UNDERSHAFT

Nat West Tower

22

N

21

20

WP William Peabody statue
JR Julius Reuter memorial
F.   Drinking fountain

OLD BROAD STREET

GRACECHURCH STREET

CORNHILL

19

18

17

THROGMORTON STREET

ANGEL COURT

Stock Exchange

2

FINCH LANE

ST. MICHAEL'S ALLEY

16

15

12

13

11

ST. PETER'S A.

PETER'S STREET

BARTHOLOMEW LANE

3

4

WP F.
Royal Exchange Bgs.

5

7

9

14

JR
F.

8

10

BALL CT.

THREADNEEDLE

Royal Exchange

1

6

CASTLE COURT

BIRCHIN LANE

no 3/4

BELL'S INN YD.

BANK OF ENGLAND

CORNHILL

GEORGE YARD

PRINCES STREET

LOMBARD

STREET

BANK

0   20   100
metres

At the Cornhill end of the paving, the canopied drinking fountain (1911) involves red Peterhead Granite, a stone very popular in London once the East Coast railway route into King's Cross had been established as a means of transport from north Aberdeenshire in the 1850's. As a red granite, it is interesting to compare it with the Trowelsworthy Granite seen earlier. Peterhead is a distinctive salmon-pink colour, this being the tone of the orthoclase feldspar crystals which also give a marked even-grained texture to the rock overall. There are no larger-than-average crystals, but a regular feature of Peterhead surfaces of any size is the occurrence of dark included fragments of the Dalradian country rock into which the granite was intruded (sometimes called 'heathen', or more formally, xenoliths).

Moving into Cornhill from the pedestrian precinct, **The Banca**

Banca Nazionale del Lavoro, Cornhill.

Nazionale del Lavoro (6) is a typical building of the Victorian High Gothic commercial style, completed in 1857. Appropriately for its present ownership, it shows many details drawn directly from the Italian palaces of Florence or Rome by the architects, the Francis brothers, who contributed several of these touches to the streets of London as we see in other walks. The Bank is of Portland Stone, recently cleaned, with a low course of grey granite at pavement level. Note how the window surrounds of each floor are of different orders or architecture—details which, with the elaborate cornice, once again display the 'freestone' qualities of Portland Stone.

On the north side of Cornhill opposite, **The Cooperative Bank**, Union Building (**7**), has much simpler lines which are more typical of the 1920's when it was built. At street level, the Bank shows two dark coloured 'granites' before passing up into walling of Portland Stone. The lowest courses are of a close-textured intensely black igneous rock which brings us back to the problem of 'Black Granite' once more. Judging from the time of construction of this Bank (1922), it is probable that the stone here came from Finland or Sweden rather than any area farther afield, the Baltic Shield being the original source of dense black stone for the trade. The other dark granite here is more normal in its character (that is, less altered and darkened by

inclusions), and from both its sombre colour tone and the swirling pattern of its feldspar minerals could be identified as coming from Aberdeenshire. In places it contains small included fragments of schist which represent the country rock into which the granite was intruded. It remains a sombre building, needing regular washing down of its black polished surfaces to obtain any effect of grandness.

On the opposite side of Cornhill, **The Union Discount Company of London (8)** achieves just this impact from the elegance of its design and the quality of its stonework after recent refurbishment and reconstruction of the entrance. Surviving from the original building are the polished granite panels at street level and the solid, turned columns attached to the frontage up to second floor level. Cornish Granite,

The Union Discount Company of London, Cornhill.

possibly from Carnmenellis, with giant white orthoclase feldspars forms the base to the columns, followed by bands of dark grey Rubislaw Granite from Aberdeen, a granite of much finer texture overall. The columns themselves are of pink Peterhead Granite showing up to good effect against the fresh white rendering of the wall surfaces. Turning to the entrance, where much new work has been done, we meet another red granite with a somewhat different character which offers some points worth noting. First, if we look at the texture we can see that the minerals are often aligned

Detail of the granite columns and mouldings of The Union Discount.

into streaked-out lenses and swirling patterns. Some panels are crossed by veins of pink feldspathic nature with occasional pods of quartz. Both of these aspects, texture and venation suggest that this rock has been subject to some metamorphism which has transformed it into a low grade gneiss. the rock is in fact Imperial Mahogany Granite from the mid-American Shield area of North Dakota—a granite which has been very popular with architects in recent years for its warm, red-brown colour and its fabric. This latter feature provides another point of interest in this building. Faced with the gneissic grain and the venation the stone fitters have exploited these features in the entrance by cutting slabs from an original block and setting them edge to edge like the pages of a book, so that kaleidoscopic patterns of impressive effect are achieved when the panels are spotlit at an angle.

We now come to **St Michael's Cornhill** (**9**), a Wren church rebuilt after the Fire of 1666, but much more extensively renovated at a later date by George Gilbert Scott (1857–60), so that what we see from Cornhill is heavily Gothicised. The entrance porch is flanked by row upon row of columns of Portland Stone overshadowed somewhat by others of Peterhead Granite. Both types are capped by limestone capitals with some of the richest three-dimensional foliage that you could find anywhere. Cleaning and renewal may have something to do with this

richness, as is certainly responsible for the pitting and yellowish patina of the stone here—an effect which causes an initial hesitation before pronouncing it 'Portland Stone' rather than one of the browner Jurassic limestones. There is no such problem, however, with the stone of the west wall of the church to St Michael's Alley, as this is white and weathered in the fashion which is unmistakeably Portland. As the stone projects in a waist-high bench, rain drips from above and the solution effects which follow have locally etched deep hollows into the surface, some of which have been clumsily patched with a stone paste of quite different hue. Nearby on the same surface, large fragments of Jurassic oyster shell stand out proud as the limestone matrix has been eaten back more rapidly than the fossil in the course of more than two centuries of local atmospheric weathering since Wren's rebuilding in 1677. 'Patching' and possible resurfacing would be a kind of sacrilege in the face of such a geological *memento mori*.

Linked to the church by a much later arch which gives access to a very peaceful courtyard is a Victorian building typical of the Chambers and Offices which were crowded into this tight area of the City (**10**). **Jamaica Buildings** (1868) has several points of geological interest, not least the fact that it is that rare thing hereabouts—a sandstone building, using the rich red stone from the New Red Sandstone of the

Mansfield area of Nottinghamshire. Large quantities of this sandstone were brought by rail to London in the latter half of the 19th century to be used as stone dressings in buildings of other types of stone, usually with the intention of producing a colour and textural contrast. A good example is St Pancras Station on the Euston Road. An inherent problem of Mansfield Stone or indeed any sandstone with a bedded character comes when the stone is dressed into pillars, pilasters or window surrounds with the long axis of the unit parallel with the original bedding. When this is done, there is a very real possibility that erosion will selectively pick out the bedding through rainwash down the surface, producing profound fissuring and spalling of the stone. Some of the effects of 'face-bedding' can be seen here in the window surrounds, as well as some too-ingenious attempts at patching which, while they got the red colour approximately right, destroyed any possible blend by including prominently dark grains of flint in the made-up paste. Clearly, some of this active weathering and decay of the stonework in this building must have arisen from the generally sunless character of this narrow alleyway.

St Michael's Alley is in fact part of a whole series of Courts and Alleys which thread a tortuous pattern between the main thoroughfares of Cornhill and Eastcheap. In 1970, this was one of the districts designated as a Conservation Area of the City in a bid to preserve this surviving fabric, not just of the London of Dickens, but of the crowded commercial heart of the London rebuilt by Wren. As the plaque on Jamaica Building records, St Michael's Alley was the site of the first Coffee House in London—'at the Sign of Pasqua Rosees Head, 1652'. Today, planning and the reconstruction of the properties in the Alley seem very much in scale and sympathy with the old and carried out in a genuine spirit of conservation. Witness for example the form of Nos. 3 and 4, two shops newly faced in rather splendid red granites, the one coarsely textured (No. 4), the other fine-grained (No. 3). Both rocks could very well be from Sweden or the Baltic Shield, but the precise provenance is unknown.

Back in Cornhill, the entrance to **The National Westminster Bank**

(**11**) is flanked by columns of grey-brown Kemnay Granite from mid-Aberdeenshire—a finer grained and browner toned granite than the Rubislaw seen earlier. The Bank foyer and interior walls are lined with a cream-coloured marble with red or purple veins giving it a richer character. These Edwardian marble surfaces together with equally fine mahogany counters and panelling, make one regret the 'modernisation' of so many Banks in recent years. The marble could be Pavonazzo or a Calacatta Marble from the general region of Carrara in the northern Apennines, but at this point it is probably as well to confess that the identification of marble is almost as difficult to a geologist as naming a sandstone. Problems lie in the variety sometimes allowed to a particular name as offered by the Trade, in the natural variation in the stone from any locality, and sometimes in a mis-identification by the Trade. We also of course have the fundamental difference over the term 'Marble'. To the Trade marble can be any stone which will take and retain a polished surface and so can include granite, lava, or limestone as much as what is marble to a geologist. To a geologist, the term has a much more restricted meaning and only covers limestones which have suffered metamorphism and been reconstituted following heating or compression.

No. 52 Cornhill, **The Gerling Globe Reinsurance Company** (**12**), is an interesting building in the Art Deco style of the 1930's. It combines panels of dark, almost black Larvikite and grey-brown Kemnay Granite from Aberdeenshire with main walls of buff coloured Italian Travertine. As we see the pale stone in the entrance surround it is easy to make out the banded nature of the rock, as well as the irregular shaped cavities which give the rock its rough texture. If we remember that travertine is a calcareous spring deposit laid down as lime-rich waters bubbled to the surface, perhaps it is easier to understand what we see. The cavities could be the trace of aquatic grasses which became encrusted with lime. These cavities are normally plugged with a lime paste when the rock is prepared for external use in buildings, producing what is termed Filled- or Stopped-Travertine.

A little further up Cornhill, we

come to **St Peter's Church (13)** which, if anything, is less conspicuous than St Michael's from street level as it is crowded out by other buildings. This is ironic in that it actually stands on one of the highest points in the City, just over 20 m OD, and with its distinctive Wren spire it might have been something of a landmark. Totally hemmed in, however, its red brick with stone dressings and some Wren details are best seen from its churchyard, reached by way of St Peter's Alley from Cornhill. The same quiet backwater affords sight of an interesting foreign limestone in the tall back wall of **Nomura House (14)**. The rock is a dull surfaced blue-grey limestone crowded with thick shelled fossil bivalves which clearly lived in communities as close-packed as oyster

Detail of the shell-bearing marble, Nomura House, St Peter's Alley Scale in cm.

beds. In some ways it is not unlike some British limestones from the Lias of the Midlands or the South West (Marston Marble comes to mind), but there is a possibility that this rock came from Portugal. Whatever its source, in this somewhat sunless corner of the churchyard the limestone has not weathered too well having lost some of its original polish and become slightly mildewed with a white efflorescence. Again, some of these changes may have been encouraged by rainwash down the sheer wall face, coupled with the extension of a limey smear from mortars fixing the slabs. No similar effect seems to have touched the panels of Terrazzo which were combined in the walling. This is an artificial stone involving small chips

of limestone, marble, or mudstone scattered evenly on to a bonding matrix of cement paste sometimes of an interesting colour contrast. The blocks when set are sliced like salami and surface-finished.

Returning to Cornhill, the premises which flank St Peter's Alley, **No. 55 Cornhill (15)**, effectively displays the characteristics of Victorian Terracotta—the smooth surface finish to the blocks, the ringing tone which comes from the dense and compact fired tile and the ability to cast details and mouldings such as those which decorate this building. Note too the satyr-like figures (or are they devils?), peering down from the gables on to St Peter's. All this was a product of the Doulton Works at Lambeth in the late 19th century—an enterprise which did much to make terracotta a popular material with architects of the time.

Another building in which terracotta plays an important role stands opposite to us, but in No. 65, **Gillet's (16)**, the material is used in conjunction with some imaginative and good-quality brickwork. Terracotta adds detail along with some attractive ceramic tile medallions. Colour contrast is another aim here in a design which represents a favourite Victorian commercial theme—the Venetian palazzo. As the building has just been cleaned and painted, the overall effect is quite striking.

Italianate facade to No. 65, Cornhill.

We have now come to the end of Cornhill and swing northwards into

Bishopsgate, drawn by the surviving buildings of the period 1890–1936 on the west side rather than the entirely new blocks of the opposite pavement which are rather short of stone. On the corner we start with a solid rock in **The Toronto Dominion Bank (17)**, the rock in question being grey-brown Kemnay Granite from the Don Valley in mid-Aberdeenshire. Best seen in the large surfaces on either side of the Cornhill entrance, a striking feature of this granite is the fabric conveyed by the elongate feldspars which amounts to a faint foliation. This could arise from movement of the melt prior to cooling, or be a consequence of mild deformation after final cooling, reflecting the position of the granite within the folded Dalradian rocks of the eastern Grampians. Another feature is the occurrence of large crystals of muscovite mica in the rock texture, which cause glistening reflections from the polished surfaces.

Compared with the Scottish-ness of the Toronto Bank there is no such certain association in what was built for **The Royal Bank of Scotland** next door in 1877 in a most imposing classical style (**18**). The rock-faced and rusticated surfaces of grey granite at pavement level are of uncertain source, but could well be Cornish from the presence of large white feldspar crystals which can be seen in spite of the rough hewn surface. The upper floors, including the massive Ionic capped columns, are of grimy Portland Stone to complete the English-ness of this building. It

is, however, no longer The Royal Bank of Scotland (1983), and in any case nationalism does not always call the tune in building stone matters.

Redevelopment at the time of writing also effects the premises next door, **Nos. 7–9 Bishopsgate (19)**, but what seems likely to survive are door surrounds and lower floor panels of rich red Swedish Bon Accord Granite from Uthammar in Central Sweden. This distinctive rock is coarsely crystalline with its large feldspar crystals often showing evidence of crushing to the extent that they are sliced through by fracture planes. The same stresses have induced a weak foliation to the rock which could allow it to be termed gneiss although its granite characteristics are still strongly evident. As often was the case with buildings of this age (1900), the strong red granite was offset by panels of dense 'Black Granite', at this date probably from a Swedish or a Finnish source. We can await the refurbishment of this building with interest.

Scandinavian rocks of a different type are prominent in the frontage to **Credit Suisse**, a newly completed building on the opposite side of Bishopsgate (**20**). The more spectacular of two stones here is a brown granite best seen at pavement level where, to the naked eye, a strongly porphyritic texture is obvious, but one in which the large feldspar phenocrysts are clearly surrounded by an additional growth of mineral matter, often of a different

'Black' and brown granite frontage, Credit Suisse, 22–24 Bishopsgate.

National Westminster Bank, Bishopsgate (Gibson's Bank)

colour. The golf-ball size of the larger feldspar crystals, and their 'Scotch-Egg' structure distinguish this brown granite from the Cornish or Shap Granites which we have seen up to now, and identify it as one of the Rapakivi Granites which outcrop in the southern margins of the Finnish Shield. The rock is Baltic Brown Granite, quarried on the shores of the Gulf of Finland, close to the border with the Soviet Union. Combined with Baltic Brown is a very dense and fine-grained 'Black Granite' of unknown source, but an effective contrast to the other stone.

From this point in Bishopsgate, in front of a very modern building of 1981, we can take stock of a very notable Victorian building of 1865. **The National Westminster Bank (21)** designed by John Gibson for the National Provincial Bank of England at the junction with Threadneedle Street was recently threatened with demolition (1971), but is now secure under a preservation order in recognition of its architectural merit. The building has been sympathetically cleaned and renewed and indeed, has new uses, all of which should cheer us when we seek to conserve. For the time of its building, this was a bank of modest size when set alongside the towering norm for Threadneedle Street. But what it lacked in stature it made good in the richness of the decoration, including its parapet crowded with allegorical figures representing Commerce, Trade and Industry, all in healthy and robust state (and in Portland Stone). Once again, in all of this we can appreciate the freestone qualities of Portland Stone and nowhere better than in the corner entrance above which stands the seal-like coat of arms of The National Provincial Bank of England, complete with a representation of the old Bishop's Gate of the City.

Just behind Gibson's Bank is the broad base from which springs the soaring 200 m high **The National Westminster Tower** rather like an Apollo rocket set upon its launching pad (**22**). While the tower itself is all glass and metal, the substantial base storeys are clad in two different granites. Towards Bishopsgate the building has a skin of silver-grey Sardinian Grey Granite from the Palaeozoic of the Sassari district in the north west of the island. What is

Sardinian Grey Granite base to The Nat. West Tower, Bishopsgate.

impressive here is the almost invisible matching of the fitted panels as well as the fact that they pass round a series of curving surfaces without a break. Notice the white and grey feldspar intergrowths, the glassy quartz and the wisps of mica which make up this equal-grained texture. The second granite of the site is the red-brown Dakota Imperial Mahogany Granite seen already in Cornhill,

which here clads the stalk-like base to the Tower. The best surfaces for study are to be found in the low walls to the Old Broad Street approach to the Tower where you gain advantage from any direct sunlight which may be available in making out the near-metamorphic colour streaking in the rock, and some of the included masses which also modify the body colour. The paved areas are of yellow brown York Stone from the Coal Measures of West Yorkshire, but if you peer in through the glass of the ground floor, you will see that the interior paving is of the buff coloured Italian Perlato Marble from the Cretaceous of western Sicily. This beautiful limestone is often crowded with fossils including bryozoans, small corals, kidney-shaped calcareous algae and broken brown fragments of thick bivalve shell. The reddish brown irregular lines which cross the surfaces are the result of pressure-solution effects which dissolved the limestone locally at the time of its' crystallisation, leaving the contacts lined with insoluble dark coloured clay.

Returning to Bishopsgate, **Hambros Bank** (**23**) is a simple building of good quality red brick with stone dressings, in contrast to the mass of surrounding Banks. Inevitably, the stone of the stone dressings is Portland Stone, which expands to make up the greater part of **Palmerston House** next door (**24**). In the recessed entrance to this building, there are wall panels of yet another 'Black Granite', but the substantial drum-section pillars which flank the doorway are of sombre grey Rubislaw Granite, showing the slightly foliated texture and the dark schist inclusions which are a regular feature of that particular granite.

From this side of the street, we gain a good impression of one of the grander commercial buildings of the late 1920's, **Hasilwood House** built by the architect Arthur Davis for the Hudson's Bay Company—a fact which explains the beaver weathervane capping the building and some of the motifs which decorate its surface (**25**). The long continuous frontage extending on either side of the entrance to the central closed courtyard is of massive blocks of Portland Stone, recently cleaned, but remaining rather yellow. At pavement level there is the customary substantial course of granite, which appears to be Cornish Granite from the presence of large white crystals of orthoclase feldspar which stand out from the axe dressed finish.

At this point, Bishopsgate suddenly widens and we come to a new tower block in **The Bank of Hong Kong**, set back from and at a slight angle to the main street (**26**). The facings to the tower and to the low walls which surround the car park area are of brilliant blue Larvikite its large feldspar crystals crowded with small dark inclusions. Equally impressive are the panels of marble used in the main concourse and foyer, the floor being of a red marble breccia with strong white calcite veins, while the walls are lined with a pale cream marble with fine grey and purple veins. The red breccia may be Breccia Pernice from Verona, while the pale marble may be Calacatta Vagli from Lucca, South of Carrara in Italy. A more restrained use of pale marble is to be seen in the banking hall of **The British Bank of the Middle East** (facing on to Bishopsgate), where what seems to be pure white Pentelic Marble from Greece is used in the window bases and flooring , whilst the inner walls and counters are of coarsely banded stopped travertine.

The broad thoroughfare of Wormwood Street leading west to London Wall is a natural break to our progress at this point, but there is reason to cross to the northern corner to examine the stone fitted to **Hornes** the Outfitters, (**27**) if only to enlarge the range of rock types which we have seen so far. At pavement level, the rocks include a brown non-metamorphosed limestone from the Carboniferous succession of the Pas de Calais which is marketed as Napoleon Marble. Close inspection of the panels which surround the windows will probably fail to find any recognisable fossils, although some of the cloudy patches may be of algal origin. This unfossiliferous character coupled with the undulose banding and figuring which sometimes looks like 'landscape marble', suggest that this was a shallow-water, possibly lagoonal lime mud, laid down close to shore in Carboniferous times. Moving up to first floor levels in the same building, we come upon two further rock types, the first of which is rather discoloured green Lake District Slate formed from the fine-grained volcanic ashes of the Borrowdale Volcanic

St. Ethelburga's Church and Hasilwood House, Bishopsgate.

Series of the central belt of the Cumbrian mountains. The other stone of the face of this building is the Italian Barge Quartzite, a buff-brown metamorphic rock from the mountains of Savoy—originally a sandstone but later altered by heat and pressure to become a fused-grain quartzite type rock, with cleavage surfaces coated with muscovite mica. This is a rock type which we see in buildings close to the Guildhall on another walk, but more widely, it is a stone which has been adopted by Trumans Brewery in their chain of public houses.

Directly opposite, **Bishop's House** (**28**), a modern concrete and glass building of 1976 mainly occupied by Barclays Bank, deserves our attention for two reasons. First, the concrete facing of the walls is vertically ridged and grooved to give a very rugged finish with the rough broken surfaces closely simulating some natural stones. Secondly, the entrance at the south east corner is lined with the bright cherry-red American Colorado Red Granite.

If we now cross Camomile Street to the south, we find another modern development making up the corner site and extending some distance down Bevis Marks. The whole complex includes shops and a pub, all framed in a stone finish which again is dominated by a vertical grooving after the style we have just seen in Bishop's House, but here on a much finer scale. What is more, the material here is not concrete but the pale buff marble Nabre-

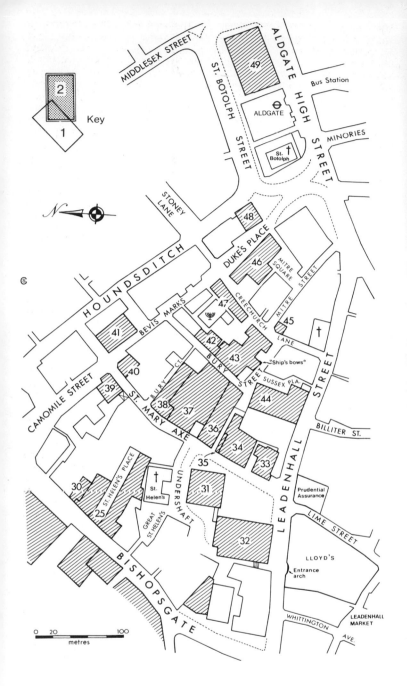

Key

2
1

N

sina, sometimes called Roman Stone, from the Cretaceous hills above Trieste. Close examination of the raised rib surfaces (which are polished) will reveal the brown shell debris which is a feature of this beautiful warm-toned marble. It seems profligate to have treated it as if it were concrete or something equally cheap. As if to compensate,

one of the shop units, **Stewart Wrightson's (29)**, offers us what could be called a geological plum in the stone to be seen in a low plinth beneath the covered entry to Wrestlers Court. On the polished surfaces of this low bench, radiate clusters of slender feldspar laths are an obvious feature of the rock. Between the clusters are patches of a dull brown hue, evenly spaced throughout. There seems little doubt that this is an alkaline igneous rock (a Foyaite) from the region of the Sierra de Monchique in the Algarve of southern Portugal. The rock is as recognisable as the Larvikites from Oslo or our own Shap Granite and from just as limited a geographical source.

Retracing our steps back down Bishopsgate, it is worthwhile pausing to look closely at the rough rubble walling of **St Ethelburga's Church (30)**, one of the few surviving mediaeval churches in London. Here we can see the rough shaped blocks of Kentish Rag which was so widely used in all the grander buildings of the City until the advent of Portland Stone in the 17th century. In many of the churches rebuilt by Wren after the Fire, whatever Kentish Rag walling that remained sound was simply encased in a skin of smooth-surfaced white limestone to provide a smooth ashlar finish. Here, the Rag remains freely visible as a grey-green sandy limestone, well-cemented and hard, speckled with green grains of glauconite, but without fossils.

Passing St Helen's Place and Hasilwood House, our route now takes us through the alley of Great St Helen's, past St Helen's Church which is as large in proportions at St Ethelburga's is small, and so into what has become one of the larger open spaces of the City. This grew from the imaginative use of a combined site for the rebuilding, as towers of reinforced concrete, of the headquarters of **Commercial Union Insurance (31)** and **P. & O. (32)** in the early 1960's. There are strong visual contrasts between the two towers, but geologically, only the Commercial Union building has details to draw us, and fortunately they are on the ground floor and can be appreciated by simply peering in through the plate glass windows. It is the floor which first catches the eye, because it is paved with slabs of Cornish granite of the Bodmin Moor type, rich in lath-shaped crystals of feldspar which give a sense of flow prior to final crystallisation. In the south west corner of floor space the sculptural study 'Striving Forces of a Sphere' has the form of two interlocking spheres of pink granite which may well be Italian Granito Rosa or something similar. The plinth on which it stands is painted to look like stone.

The open space about the base of the two towers now allows us half perspective views of the surrounding buildings of Leadenhall Street and St Mary Axe which were impossible before, when the area was the intersection of two Portland Stone canyons. To the south, one of the canyon walls survived until 1980. Then Sir Edwin Cooper's massive Lloyds Bank of 1928 was demolished to make way for a redevelopment of the Lloyds site. Only the scheduled grand arched entrance of the north west corner remains. What goes up in its place will probably be faced in white Portland Stone, but can hardly seem so solid as, say, **The Prudential Assurance** building on the opposite corner. This has the gleaming whiteness we see in 1930's buildings such as Senate House, or Shell Mex House off The Strand. Turning to look east, St Mary Axe has the church of **St Andrew Undershaft (33)** close to its junction with Leadenhall Street, and again space allows us to appreciate how its plan was originally very much dictated by the space available between pre-existing premises. Its tower, west-end gable and porch are all capped by smooth-dressed Portland Stone, while the main wall surfaces show the same stone in a rough bolstered finish. This last surface remains begrimed and mottled in colour compared with the cappings. At a time when cleaning is so universal a process, it may seem perverse to suggest that perhaps one or two buildings like St Andrews might well be left untouched, if only to remind us what was once a general condition in Central London. As it is, the rough-dressed surfaces would be particularly difficult to clean and there is a sense in which the darkness adds to the three dimensional quality of the structure seen from the square. One further geological detail of the church is worth noting. The low walling to the entrance off St Mary Axe is capped by a deeply etched current-bedded Middle Jurassic limestone, possibly from north Oxfordshire, which having decayed, has at some time been atrociously badly patched with a discoloured paste of cement. This should be a lesson to us all.

Facing the church is **Cayzer House (34)**, an office block of 1880 which becomes geologically interesting at first floor level. From here upwards, we can see stonework of a

Walling of weathered oolite, St Andrew Undershaft Church.

rich ginger-brown colour which tells us that this is a building of Bath Stone—a material of good repute almost everywhere, but never quite successful in London. Nos. 2–4 St Mary Axe are also part of Cayzer House, and here new development has introduced surfaces of the striking black and white marble known as Bleu Belge. This rock comes from the folded and deformed Carboniferous succession of the Meuse Valley. The sense of movement involved in the deformation is conveyed by the tension gash veins which you can trace across these surfaces. More stone of a deformed and metamorphosed character can be seen at pavement level where tablets of greenish schist form the frontage.

The Halifax Building Society (35) shows another metamorphic rock type in the silvery-grey Otta Schist from the mountains of central Norway south of Trondheim. In other buildings of London, this same rock is seen in its rough-riven finish, with the elongate crystals of hornblende sticking out like matchsticks from the surface. Here, the surfaces have been smoothened to a semi-matt finish which has the strange effect of seeming to make the rock translucent. The point of interest remains the size and slenderness of the hornblende crystals which must have grown within the rock as it was altered. In this building the schist is matched with a blue-grey, fine grained granite which may be from the Dalbeattie area of the Southern Uplands of Scotland:

Williams & Glyn's Bank (36), offers several large surface areas of Ashburton or Torquay Marble. This is a genuine marble of Devonian age from the British Isles where the deformation is conveyed by the shape of the contained fossils, and the tendency for the dark surfaces to be crossed by red calcite veins. The most prominent fossils are colonial corals which stand out pale against the dark mud of the body of the limestone, but equally numerous are crinoid ossicles and fragments of brachiopods. As a stone the Torquay Limestone is excellent for interior work, where it retains its polish and rich dark tone, but externally used, it soon tends to lose surface and become disappointingly dull if not treated regularly.

Proceeding down St Mary Axe, we now come to the impressive frontage of **The Baltic Exchange (37)**. Built in 1900–03, the notable feature must be the solid masonry involving a blood-red granite up to first floor level, including massive pillars to the entrance. The rock is Swedish Virgo Granite from either Gravefors or Vanevik, a stone which became very popular in Victorian times for its rich regal colour, unmatched by any British granite worked at that time. A distinctive feature of the rock is the intensely blue or violet colour of the quartz grains in the rock, a colour which may be produced by internal light reflections produced by crushing of the mineral within the granite. The magnificent glassy polish of this stone in The Exchange allows us to make out the constituent minerals with a hand lens.

Sadly. St Mary Axe is a narrow street, and west or north west facing, which means that direct sunlight rarely plays upon this building, otherwise, it would have surely become one of the most celebrated of the City.

If the exterior is grand, and appropriately Scandinavian, it is worth-while seeking permission to slip inside the Exchange on a weekday if only to see the richness of the interior hall, lined with those Antique Marbles which were so much favoured by the Edwardians. Most of the stone here is of a strongly-veined Arebescato or Paonazzetto type from Italy, but there are also panels and pillars of green ophicalcite, Green Marble from Central Sweden to maintain the Baltic connection. The day to day business of the Baltic Exchange is to organise the shipping of cargo by sea and air, and it is worth reflecting that to the traditional commodities there now must be added an increased traffic in building stone from foreign and distant places.

The Baltic Exchange, St Mary Axe.

The headquarters of **The Chamber of Shipping** next door (**38**), is a building modernised in 1964 by Burnet, Tait & Partners. Beneath the hardwood coat of arms and the anchor chains, the plate glass front allows us to see the foyer walling of grey Grigio Fiorito Marble from the Devonian of Udine in the Italian Tyrol. In strong contrast to this dark grey limestone riven by white calcite veins, the flooring is of white Carrara Venato Marble from Italy. Finally, the steps and entrance paving from St Mary Axe, are of fine grained grey granite, which may be the same Hantergantick Granite that we saw in The Stock Exchange (stop **2**).

On the north pavement of the street, extending to the junction with Bevis Marks, a large new block, **No. 61, St Mary Axe** (**39**) gives a strong impression of being of mirror-glass and concrete, when in fact the 'concrete' is once again the attractive Nabresina Marble in panels which have been scored vertically as if to disguise the fact. Natural stone comes back strongly in **The Bank of Greece** on the opposite corner (**40**), where the stone is Golden Carioca Granite from the Campo Grande district of Brazil, just to the west of Rio de Janeiro. As with most igneous rocks it is the feldspar minerals which impart the general colour to the rock overall. Here, the feldspars have been sericitised and altered to an opaque yellow ochre colour within which the hornblende and mica add touches of darker hue. Looking at the polished slabs, you can see that here there is a swirling pattern of minerals which tell that the granite has at some stage been deformed and a fabric overprinted upon it which gives it a gneissic texture. As it is one of the 'older' granites of the Precambrian Brazilian Shield, this is to be expected.

There has been much change in Bevis Marks in recent years, and older buildings have been cleared to make way for new. Surviving on the east side is **Chatsworth House** (**41**), premises with large surface areas of polished serpentinite facing on to the street. In these surfaces we can readily see the intensely shattered and broken nature of this interesting rock type which truly represents the deep foundation layers of mountain belts such as the Alps. At depth, basic and ultrabasic rocks are altered to masses of the mineral chlorite, magnetite and ores—hence the rich green colours which prevail in serpentinites. The other aspect which is constant is the richness of the rock in calcite veining—the feature which gives the serpent-skin appearance referred to in the popular name for the rock. In Chatsworth House, we see again the skill of the stone fitters in quartering the blocks to produce the diamond-form patterns from the veined slabs. Much of the Serpentinite used in Britain comes from either north west Italy around Turin or Aosta, or from Greece north of Salonika.

Turning back along Bury Street, on the left hand side there is a a new building occupied by Rank-Xerox (**42**) faced with an interesting red granite. The rock extends throughout the floors and around the bowed-out windows in surfaces which allow us to see that it has a texture which is not unlike that of the Rapakivi Granite which we saw in Credit Suisse in Bishopsgate, particularly in the large zoned feldspars which stand out against the strongly coloured groundmass. I am indebted to the architects Hildebrand & Glicker for the information that this red granite is in fact from Austin in Texas, demonstrating the wide range of sources which are liable to come into stone fitting in London today. In the United States the stone is known as Texas Pink Granite and geologically it represents the Precambrian basement emerging in the Llano Uplift from beneath the Mesozoic cover rocks of Texas.

No. 10 Bury Street, Texas Pink Granite.

Continuing down Bury Street, the next building may at first seem rather dull and sombre in its tone with Rank-Xerox. It is, however, a building of great interest both architecturally and geologically. Once occupied by The National Employers Federation (**43**), it was built in 1914

by the Dutch architect Berlage for a Dutch shipping company—a fact which explains the very individual detail of its frontage which will be mentioned later. The whole structure

Ship's Bow detail in Larvikite, Bury Street.

is based upon a massive foundation of very three dimensional slabs of Larvikite, polished and smooth, and almost black in tone. True to type, the stone shows the iridescent feldspars which always identify this Norwegian syenite. Combined with this rich stone base, the walling of the upper floors is of a bluish-tinged white ceramic tile. This material picks out the strong vertical elements in the design as continuous columns separating the tall windows. Following Bury Street around, we come to the south face of the building and its main entrance from a small courtyard. At the angle of the court we see the trade-mark of the original owners—the bow and superstructure of a pre-First World War Liner, complete with a stiff bow wave, all fashioned from solid Larvikite. The visual effect coming into this quiet backwater of a street from the slab fronts and busy traffic of Leadenhall Street must be one of the architectural surprises of London.

What is both a coincidence and a contrast emerges when we look at the rear of the premises of **The Bank of Credit and Commerce**, the Leadenhall House of Leadenhall Street (**44**). This is a tower block of brown glass and what looks at first like concrete. In fact the slate-grey slabs are actually the same Larvikite seen in the Federation building, but here, in the modern building treated with what is termed 'flame-finish'. Although this renders the surface matt, the tell-tale large feldspars still flash with brilliance in oblique light to identify the rock.

At the junction of Creechurch Lane and Mitre Street, **Cree House (45)**, is a Victorian commercial building of 1880 surviving with only minor changes. It is principally or orange-red bricks and includes panels of the same bricks moulded and rubbed to form flower decorations running across the entire frontage in bands, culminating in the grapevines and orange trees at the corner angle. The arches capping the windows show the familiar polychrome effect achieved by setting blocks of Red Mansfield Sandstone alongside yellow oolite from the Jurassic in wedge-shaped blocks.

International House Creechurch Lane (**46**) is of Portland Stone in its usual form, but the base which we would normally expect to be granite, turns out to be concrete, rendered with a strew of sand grains to produce the impression of granite. Such economy did not prevail when the Aldgate—Bevis Marks road improvements were carried out in 1979. The kerbstones, including the neatly curved sections were fashioned from silver-grey Hantergantick Granite from Cornwall. **Arthur Castle House (47)** on the opposite corner of the Lane is equally genuine in the facings of rich orange-toned Sardinian Beige Granite—the textural twin of the Sardinian Grey seen in the National Westminster Tower in Old Broad Street and Bishopsgate. Here, the beige colour of the feldspar is responsible for the overall colour of the whole rock.

Once into Dukes Place (linking Bevis Marks with Aldgate High Streed), the eye is immediately caught by the outline of **Irongate House (48)**, a building completed by Fitzroy, Robinson & Partners in 1978. With space at ground level surrounded by strong stone-clad pillars, the windows of all floors are recessed between strong horizontal and vertical stonework. As you approach the building and focus upon that stonework, you become aware of the deformed metamorphic texture of the stone and begin to recognise

gneissic banding such as you might see on the sea-washed rocks of the Hebrides. This predominantly red gneissic rock is Parys Granite which comes from the Vredefort Dome area of the Transvaal of the South African Pre-Cambrian Shield. For several reasons this attractive rock, seldom if ever seen elsewhere in London, could make Irongate House something of a place of pilgrimage for geologists in London.

Irongate House (Parys Granite), Bevis Marks, Aldgate.

To complete the walk with yet more evidence of the cosmopolitan character of stone supply today, it is only necessary to skirt the old Wren church of **St Botolph (49)** and turn into Aldgate High Street. Here, beyond the entrance to Aldgate Tube Station, we come to **Sedgwick House (50)** which combines two granites of contrasting colour. The paler of the two is Sardinian Beige Granite from Sassari, seen a moment ago in Bevis Marks and Creechurch Lane. The second granite is the red-brown Canadian rock Rivière à Pierre Granite from the southern limits of Quebec Province close to the United States border. This area of south Quebec is responsible for almost 80% of the granite currently exported from Canada, large quantities of which come to Britain. The rock is from intrusions punched into the folded Ordovician and Silurian rocks of the northern Appalachian Mountains, and is of Devonian age, making it of the same general age as our own

Shap Granite. As seen here, the Canadian granite is coarsely crystalline and even-grained, although some of the pink feldspars do stand out as being slightly larger than the groundmass. Here, the prevailing colour is red-brown, but other examples from the same area are markedly more grey, as seen in Maples, Tottenham Court Road, but that is another story, and another walk.

Ancient and Modern; the towers of the Stock Exchange and the National Westminster Bank, above the pediment of the Royal Exchange.

REFERENCES

Including titles referred to in the text and others which back up the general themes of the walks accounts.

BLATCH, M. 1978. *A guide to London's Churches*, 1–434, Constable.

BYRON, A. 1981. *London Statues—a guide to London's outdoor statues and sculpture*. 1–433, Constable.

CRAWFORD, D. 1976. *The City of London—its Architectural Heritage*, 1–143, Woodhead-Faulkner/Commercial Union.

ELSDEN, J. V. & J. A. HOWE, 1923. *The Stones of London*, 1–205, Colliery Guardian, London Ltd.

FAWCETT, J. 1976. Save the City—a conservation study of the City of London, 81–90, *S.P.A.B.*

HARRIS, J. 1982. London's Square Peg?, 98–100, *Country Life.*

KEEN, D. H. 1981. The Stones of St Paul's, *Circular 824*, p. 9, Geologists' Association, London.

KUTCHNER, A. 1976. Save the City—a conservation study of the City of London, 161–165, *S.P.A.B.*

—— 1978. *Looking at London—illustrated walks through a changing city*, 1–128, *Thames & Hudson.*

LLOYD, D. 1976. Save the City—a conservation study of the City of London, 1–24, 32–43, 101–113., *S.P.A.B.*

McKEAN, C. & T. JESTICO, 1976. Guide to modern buildings in London, 1–109., Academy Editions, London.

PEVSNER, N. 1962/1973. City of London, in *Buildings of England, Penguin Books,* London (1st & 2nd editions).

SERVICE, A. 1977. *Edwardian Architecture,* 1–216, Thames & Hudson.

STAMP, G. & C. AMERY. 1980. Victorian Buildings of London, 1837–1887, 1–175, *Architectural Press London.*

SUMMERSON, J. 1976. *The Architecture of Victorian London,* University Press, Virginia.

WILSON, E. 1981. Manx Limestone and the steps of St Paul's 10–11, *Circular 823,* Geologists' Association, London.

—— 1981. The Stones of St Paul's, 8–9, *Circular 824,* Geologists' Association, London.

GLOSSARY

ACID ROCKS: igneous rocks relatively rich in silica to the extent of having free quartz as a component mineral (granite is an Acid Rock).

ASHLAR: a term in description of masonry meaning a smooth surface-finish, with fine joints. Even-grained, well-cemented stones, either sandstones or limestones, allow such a finish.

AXE-DRESSED (or HAMMER-DRESSED): a term from masonry work meaning a pecked or rough surface-finish, giving an impression of rugged strength.

BASIC ROCKS: igneous rocks relatively poor in silica, and so normally lacking free quartz as a component mineral (gabbro and basalt are Basic Rocks).

BATH STONE: a Middle Jurassic limestone (usually an oolite) of rich orange-brown colour. The traditional building stone of Bath and Bristol.

BEDDING: a natural layering in rocks of sedimentary origin reflecting short breaks in deposition. The natural plane of parting in most rocks.

BIOCLASTIC: a descriptive term implying that a rock is made up of calcareous shell debris, or natural growths broken down into sediment particles.

CARBONIFEROUS: a period of geological time, c. 360–285 m.y.; a system.

CALEDONIAN: a mountain building period recognised by geologists as occurring towards the end of the Lower Palaeozoic between 480 and 350 m.y.. Responsible for the Grampian Highlands of Scotland, and the mountains of Wales and the Lake District.

CHAMPFER: an architectural term for a surface formed when a squared angle is cut away (common in door- and window surrounds).

CLEAVAGE: a platy structure in fine grained metamorphic rocks, induced by stress during deformation. Often confused with natural bedding.

COAL MEASURES: a late Carboniferous time period during which the coal bearing rocks of Britain and Europe were formed.

CORNICE: an architectural term for a moulded projection which can cap a wall, usually at roof or floor levels.

CRETACEOUS: a period of geological time, best known for the familiar rock type Chalk, developed extensively across Western Europe c. 70–65 m.y.

DALRADIAN: a rock sequence of Precambrian to Lower Palaeozoic age, making up the greater part of the Grampian Highlands.

DEVONIAN: a period of geological time, recognised in its fullest development in the country of Devon, c. 400–360 m.y.

DIORITE: a coarse grained igneous rock, composed of plagioclase feldspar, hornblende, and biotite mica. Usually quartz-free, and dark in colour.

DOLERITE: a medium-grained, basic igneous rock. Dolerite is the rock type of most intrusive sills, and has the same composition as the lava basalt.

EXFOLIATION: a weathering habit in stone whereby crusts flake off from surfaces like skins from an onion.

FELDSPAR: an important group of rock-forming minerals present in all igneous rocks. Alumino-silicates of potassium, sodium, or calcium; typical members of the group are orthoclase (K-rich), albite (Na-rich) and anorthite (Ca-rich).

GABBRO: a coarse grained basic igneous rock, similar in grain size to granite. Lacking free quartz, but rich in pyroxene; gabbros are invariably dark in colour. Altered gabbros are the rocks most often referred to as 'Black Granite'.

GLAUCONITE: a pale-to-dark green potash-rich clay mineral, commonly found as distinct grains in sedimentary rocks. Formed only in marine conditions, it is the colouring agent in 'greensands'.

GNEISS: a strongly banded and coarse-grained metamorphic rock, recognised by its alternate layers of dark and light coloured minerals.

GRANITE: an acid igneous rock, coarsely crystalline and light-coloured on account of the high proportion of free quartz and feldspar contained. Principal minerals are orthoclase feldspar, quartz, hornblende, muscovite and biotite micas.

GREENSAND: both the name of a rock type (a sandstone containing the green mineral, glauconite), and stratigraphical units within the Cretaceous succession of southern England.

HERCYNIAN: a period of mountain-building occurring towards the end of Carboniferous time, responsible for the folding of the rocks of south west England and South Wales. The granites of Devon and Cornwall were intruded late in this period.

IGNEOUS ROCKS: rocks formed by cooling from a hot original melt (from the Latin, *ignis*—fire).

JURASSIC: a period of geological time, the source of many excellent building stones, mainly limestones; c. 213–144 m.y.

KAOLINITISED: an alteration of feldspar minerals to a clay-mineral end product, kaolinite; a source of kaolin.

MARBLE: (i) a trade name for limestones, but sometimes also igneous rocks, which can be polished and which retain that polish. (ii) a geological term for a limestone which has been altered by heat and/or pressure to the extent that its calcium carbonate has been recrystallised.

METAMORPHISM: processes of alteration of an original rock type into something different, by agencies including heat and/or pressure: thus clays become slates; limestones, marbles.

MICA: a rock-forming mineral with a flat, platy habit. There are two main varieties; muscovite mica is silvery and transparent; biotite mica is dark brown or black. Present in many igneous rocks as a primary mineral; in sediments as a derived mineral.

OLIVINE: a rock-forming mineral group; orthosilicates of iron (Fe) and magnesium (Mg), hence the term ferromagnesian for this type of mineral along with hornblende and pyroxene. Olivine is present in basic and ultrabasic igneous rocks (e.g. basalt)

OOLITE: a variety of limestone with a distinctive 'cod's roe' texture. The component grains are coated with casings of lime to an even grain size. (Bath Stone and some Portland Stone can be oolitic).

ORTHOCLASE: a rock-forming mineral of the feldspar group; the potash (K) feldspar. Present in acid igneous rocks such as granite.

ORDOVICIAN: a period of geological time, a system, c. 500–438 m.y.

PALAEOZOIC: an era of geological time, literally meaning 'ancient life'. Comprises the older systems of geological time which are fossil-bearing. c. 600–248 m.y.

PILASTER: an architectural term for a vertical, projecting column or pillar attached to a wall surface.

PORPHYRY: a rock in the terminology of classical antiquity which possessed a combination of rich colour (usually purple) with a mineral texture which made it attractive when fashioned into columns or ornaments. Geologically, a rock with a texture involving large, well-formed crystals, set against a background of finer grained character.

PORTLAND STONE: a dense creamy-white limestone of Upper Jurassic age, widely used in public buildings in Britain. Virtually all Portland Stone originates from Portland Island south of Weymouth on the Dorset Coast.

PRECAMBRIAN: a vast extent of geological time, preceding a period known as the Cambrian, which contains the earliest commonly occurring fossils; pre-600 m.y.

QUARTZITE: a tough, durable stone, entirely composed of the mineral quartz, and in which the grains are welded together more effectively than in most sandstones. Most quartzites are to a degree metamorphic rocks.

ROACH: a cavity-rich variant of Portland Stone, rough-textured.

RUSTIFICATION: an architectural term for a treatment of masonry, aimed to produce a ruggedness to a surface.

SCHISTS: a metamorphic rock with a strongly foliated (or 'leaved') character, rich in the mineral mica, which is in part responsible for the foliation. Originally, a shale or mudstone.

SERPENTINITE: a much-altered ultrabasic igneous rock, in which meta-morphism has altered the ferromagnesian minerals to the fibrous end-product serpentine, and platy chlorite. A rock type criss-crossed by prominent veins. Usually dark green or almost black, the veins, white, the resulting contrasts give the serpent-skin lustre, and the source of the name.

SYENITE: a coarse grained igneous rock, rich in potash feldspar and hornblende, but usually poor in quartz. (e.g. Larvikite)

TISBURY STONE: a buff-coloured limestone, often speckled with grains of glauconite. Quarried in Wiltshire for Salisbury Cathedral.

TRAVERTINE: a calcareous spring deposit, full of cavities and voids. Travertine is mainly of young geological times (Tertiary-Recent).

TRIASSIC: a period of geological time, named in Europe for its invariable division into three, well-defined parts. c. 248–213 m.y.

ULTRABASIC: igneous rocks poorer in silica than Basic Rocks (q.v.)

XENOLITH: literally a 'foreign' rock; a term used for a displaced fragment of an older rock incorporated into a younger.

For other definitions refer to *The Penguin Dictionary of Geology* by D. G. Whitten with J. R. V. Brooks, 1983.